Essential

Madeira

by
NIGEL TISDALL

Nigel Tisdall is an experienced travel writer
who contributes to many newspapers and magazines.
He has written guide books to a variety of European
destinations including Brittany, Andalusia and the
Canary Islands.

AA

Produced by AA Publishing

Written by Nigel Tisdall
Peace and Quiet section
by Paul Sterry
Original photography by Peter
Baker

Edited, designed and produced
by AA Publishing. Maps ©
The Automobile Association 1994

Distributed in the United Kingdom
by AA Publishing, Norfolk House,
Priestley Road, Basingstoke,
Hampshire, RG24 9NY.

© The Automobile Association
1994
Reprinted March 1995

A CIP catalogue record for this
book is available from the British
Library.

ISBN 0 7495 0713 6

Published by AA Publishing,
which is a trading name of
Automobile Association
Developments Limited, whose
registered office is Norfolk House,
Priestley Road, Basingstoke,
Hampshire, RG24 9NY.
Registered number 1878835.

Colour separation: BTB Colour
Reproduction Ltd, Whitchurch,
Hampshire

Printed by: Printers Trento, S.R.L.,
Italy

*Front cover picture: Overlooking
Funchal*

Contents

This book employs a simple rating system to help choose which places to visit:

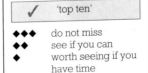

✓	'top ten'

♦♦♦   do not miss
♦♦   see if you can
♦   worth seeing if you have time

Introduction and Background

INTRODUCTION

An 'Atlantic Pearl', a 'Floating Flower-pot', 'God's Botanical Gardens' – these descriptions of Madeira have come a long a way since the island first appeared on a Genoese map of 1351 with the simple label 'Isola della Lolegname', Italian for the 'Island of Wood'. Ever since its colonisation by Portuguese settlers in the early 15th century, the Madeiran archipelago has been the happy recipient of much praise. Its earliest admirers were the merchants from Lisbon who established profitable sugar plantations on the islands, worked by slaves brought over from North Africa. Funchal, the Madeiran capital, bears witness to the fortunes made from this white gold in the form of the five sugar loaves on its coat of arms, and in the splendid 15th and 16th century Flemish paintings acquired during its lucrative trade with Flanders, which now hang in its Museum of Sacred Art.

Madeiran Wine

Even though one or two sugar mills continue to produce molasses on Madeira today, many of the island's terraces had already been given over to another money spinning crop – vines – by the 17th century. Madeira is probably best known for its eponymous fortified wine, originally called malmsey, and its dusty bottles have a compelling history. Among its many devotees none can surpass the pioneering enthusiasm of the Duke of Clarence who, facing execution in the Tower of London in

Florid Madeira

1478, demanded that he be drowned in a butt of malmsey.

Madeiran wine has a variety and distinction that surprises those unfamiliar with it. Not only does it taste good, it travels well and has a formidable longevity. In 1950 Sir Winston Churchill, one of the island's many famous visitors, had the rare privilege of being served a bottle of 1792 Bual – a wine made, as he pointed out to his guests, when Marie Antoinette was still alive. Few of us can afford such luxuries, but a glass of chilled Sercial on the hotel balcony as the sun sets over the Atlantic is a far from disagreeable experience.

Tourism and Madeira

Like its wine, Madeira has pedigree. Tourists have been coming here since the mid-19th century, especially the British, who liked to stop over en route to and from their colonies around the world. They founded the island's first luxurious hotels, established its wicker and embroidery industries and cultivated its vineyards and gardens. It was an Englishman,

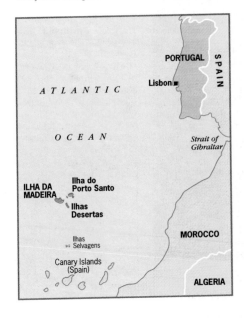

looking for a speedy means of getting to the office from his hilltop *quinta* (estate), who created what has become the island's best-known tourist attraction, the Monte toboggan ride. Until the construction of its airports in the1960s, visitors to Madeira arrived by passenger ship (and, for a romantic period in the 1950s, by flying boat) – thus preserving the island's leisured, upmarket atmosphere long after other holiday resorts had succumbed to brasher forces.

Cruise liners still call in to Funchal harbour for a day or two as part of their Atlantic voyages, but the majority of the island's visitors now arrive by air, many of them seeking refuge from the dreary rain and snow of the northern European winter. Like their predecessors, they are drawn to Madeira by its mild sub-tropical climate, its long-standing reputation for hospitality and by tales of its stunning landscape and flora. If you are such a visitor, you will not be disappointed – particularly if you make the effort to get into the mountains and valleys behind Funchal, rather than spending all of your time in the island's capital.

Nature's Profusion

The island of Madeira may only be 35 miles by 12 (56km by 19), but it rises abruptly from the sea to peaks that are 6,000ft (1,830m) or more in height. In winter these can be capped with snow – something of a treat for the fun-loving Madeirans, who like nothing better than to drive back down to Funchal with a snowman on the sunroof.

Wherever you go, Madeira has numerous *miradouros* (viewpoints) and picnic sites where you can look out over a countryside that ranges from the stupendously raw to the painstakingly cultivated. Fringed with cliffs that rise sheer from the sea, Madeira's coastline has a wild, brutal aspect that is at odds with the serene terraced valleys just a short way inland, whose slopes have been laboriously sculpted by generations of farmers. Here nature stands firmly corrected, with steep slopes cut and divided into ambitious tiers of tiny fields that nurse a profusion of crops, including vegetables and fruit trees.

Architectural grandeur in Funchal

The famous Monte toboggan ride

Venture into the Madeiran interior and you will discover further surprises and contrasts. Here there is austere moorland, remote mountain passes and thickly forested valleys that would appear to have remained undisturbed for centuries – save for the thin watery line of a *levada* cutting through the trees, part of the unique and audacious network of irrigation channels that span the island and which now make for such excellent walks.

Besides ancient laurel forests and a rich variety of native species, the countryside and gardens of Madeira have many flowers, shrubs and trees that have been successfully transplanted from around the globe. Plants that those of us who live in colder climates struggle to grow on window-sills or in conservatories thrive here with dismaying ease, and it is not uncommon to see prized flowers, such as poinsettias, growing as tall as a man and being used nonchalantly as a peg for drying plastic carrier bags.

Unhurried Idyll

However brief your stay, you will find there is far more to Madeira than a sherry-like drink. It is not just one island – the three enigmatic Ilhas Desertas (Desert Isles) lie some 19 miles (30km) to the southeast, while the larger island of Porto Santo can boast one of the few unspoilt beaches in Europe. Despite being 600 miles (960km) south of Lisbon. Madeira is now firmly in touch with the modern world, an integral part of Portugal and a far-flung corner of the European Community. At the same time it remains an unhurried idyll of simple whitewashed churches, ancient yellow and blue taxis and verandahs where the whiff of colonial days lingers on. Here you can listen to the fishmonger selling his heap of ugly-faced *espada* fish, taste exotic fruits brought from around the world and sip a wine that was used to toast the signing of the American Declaration of Independence. And, if you have the good fortune to be here on New Year's Eve, Madeira's greatest day of celebration, you will find 300,000 coloured light bulbs illuminating the streets of Funchal and a night sky filled with a radiant umbrella of fireworks.

BACKGROUND

The Madeiran archipelago lies 380 miles (608km) west of Morocco, and 260 miles (416km) north of the Canary Islands. The largest island is the green and mountainous Madeira, 285 square miles (738 square km) in area and with a shape not unlike the hulk of a storm-battered caravel, one of those sturdy ships that the Portuguese explorers of the 15th century used in their voyages of discovery. Some 23 miles (37km) to the north-east is the island of Porto Santo, only 41 square miles (106 square km) in area, with a low-lying, arid landscape that is the complete opposite of that found on Madeira.

THE MADEIRAN ARCHIPELAGO

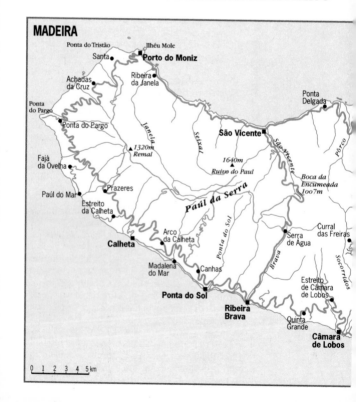

Two further groups of islands complete the archipelago. Ten miles (16km) southeast of Madeira, and easily visible from its south coast, lie the three Ilhas Desertas – Ilhéu Chão, Deserta Grande and Bugio. Despite their proximity and size – Deserta Grande rises to 1,571 feet (479m) – they have hardly any soil or fresh water and they are therefore virtually uninhabited (except for the occasional visiting naturalist). Equally inhospitable, and 135 miles (216km) south from Madeira, are the well-named Ilhas Selvagens (the Wild Islands). Although closer to the Spanish Canaries, they are under Portuguese jurisdiction and consist of two groups of rocky islets of which the largest, Selvagem Grande, is only 3 miles (5km) in circumference. Both groups of islands are now protected as nature reserves.

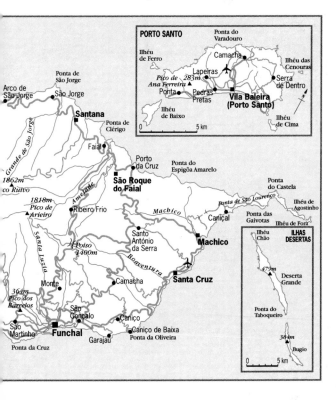

BACKGROUND

Sheer cliffs rising out of the Atlantic

Landscape

The Madeiran islands, like the nearby Azores and Canary Islands, are volcanic in origin and at least 20 million years old. Their present shape has been determined by deep erosion rather than eruption. A central range of mountains runs east-west across the length of Madeira and from this numerous ridges and ravines project seawards to the coast, often culminating in high cliffs. In the west two deep ravines, one leading north of Ribeira Brava and the other south from São Vicente, appear to be doing their utmost to cut the island in two. Beyond these, to the west, is the Paúl da Serra, the largest of several high plateaux that help temper the island's see-saw terrain. In the centre of Madeira a cluster of high mountains poke through the clouds, including the spectacular and accessible peaks of Pico Ruivo (6,106ft/1,862m) and Pico do Arieiro (5,963ft/1,818m). East of these the landscape is more relaxed, with hills and valleys tumbling down towards the southeast coast. In the northeastern corner of Madeira a narrow dribble of land known as Ponta de São Lourenço extends east into the sea.

Agriculture

Madeira is blessed with an equable sub-tropical climate, abundant water and fertile soil. Over the last five centuries its inhabitants have worked, often with great ingenuity and perseverance, to make their precipitous island agriculturally viable. Today there is hardly a slope on Madeira that has not been transformed into a staircase of green fields. These *poisos*, or terraces, which can be found in the most unlikely recesses of a valley, are supported by dry-stone walls that allow the land to drain but prevent erosion of the soil. In many cases the rich red earth you see will have been carried up by hand from the river beds below – most of the cultivable land on Madeira is too steep for the use of machinery or even of beasts of burden. Water is brought to these terraces from mountain springs by a complicated pattern of irrigation channels known as *levadas*. Their construction began with the arrival of the island's first settlers, and they now run for some 1,335 miles (2,136km), of which 25 miles (40km) is through tunnels. Maintenance work on some of the more inaccessible *levadas* is still carried out by the only practicable means – suspending workers

Working the terraces in time – honoured fashion

on long ropes from the mountains and cliffs above. Water is also a valuable source of power; once used to drive sugar mills, it now provides the island with hydro-electricity. Sugar cane, vines and bananas have always been the island's principal export crops – the amount of land given to each being determined by the prevailing economic winds abroad. Potatoes, onions, cabbages, tomatoes and a variety of beans, cereals and fruit trees are cultivated for domestic consumption. Cattle are generally kept indoors in *palheiros*, small huts that were once thatched but are now increasingly covered with corrugated tin or, occasionally, by terracotta tiles.

Porto Santo

In contrast to Madeira, the island of Porto Santo is flat and dry, its landscape punctuated by a set of volcanic peaks of which the highest, Pico do Facho, reaches 1,696 feet (517m). Here you will find grassy slopes grazed by sheep and cattle, donkeys at work in the fields and hills crowned with windmills – both ancient towers with canvas sails built to grind corn and the sleek modern propellers now used for generating electricity. Porto Santo receives little rain and in summer has the parched appearance of semi-desert. Once covered in dragon trees, the island now has little natural vegetation – the processes of desertification were unwittingly accelerated when Portuguese settlers introduced rabbits to the island. All this is redeemed, though, by the presence of a 4½-mile (7-km) curving stretch of sandy beach along the island's southern shore.

History

While legends, early maps and mariners' tales suggest that chance visits were paid to the archipelago in preceding centuries, Madeira was officially discovered in 1418 by the Portuguese navigators João Gonçalves Zarco and Tristão Vaz Teixeira. Sailing south to explore the West African coastline, they were blown west by violent storms, eventually finding shelter on an island they gratefully called Porto Santo (Holy Port). Their discovery was the first of many triumphs for Prince Henry the Navigator, whose passion for expansionist

Zarco, the Portuguese navigator who found Madeira

seafaring laid the foundations for Portugal's Golden Age. Two years later Zarco and Teixeira returned to discover a second, larger island, which was then covered with thick forest so they named it Ilha da Madeira, Portuguese for the 'Island of Wood'. Unlike the nearby Canary Islands, no sign of any pre-existing or indigenous population has ever been found on Madeira.

By 1425 settlement of the islands was underway, with great fires lit to clear the trees so that lucrative plantations of sugar cane, brought from Sicily, could be established. The new land was divided into three captaincies: Zarco took Funchal and Teixeira Machico, while Bartolomeu Perestrello became the first governor of Porto Santo. His daughter, Filipa Moniz, later married Christopher Columbus, who visited the islands at various times between 1478 and 1484 to buy sugar on behalf of merchants in Lisbon.

The early colonists also brought vines to Madeira, including the sweet *malvoisie* grape from Crete, from which the island's celebrated wine, originally known as malvasia or malmsey, is derived. By 1452 slaves were being shipped over from the Canaries and Africa. Their labour played a vital part in the construction of the terraces and *levadas* that allowed farmers to make efficient use of the island's fertile soil.

Christopher Columbus visited Madeira to buy sugar

Defences

By the start of the 16th century, the city of Funchal had around 5,000 citizens, many of them European merchants working in the sugar trade. Walls, ramparts and fortresses were built as protection against the frequent attacks from pirates, but these often proved inadequate. A permanent lookout was kept on Madeira's mountain tops and warning bonfires were lit if raiders were sighted so that the islanders had time to flee inland.

One of the worst raids took place on 3 October 1566, when over 1,000 French pirates ran amok for 16 days, looting furnishings and silver from the island's mansions and churches and killing some 300 Madeirans. This was the year that the nuns of the Convento de Santa Clara first took refuge in a remote, crater-like valley 11½ miles (18km) north of Funchal, now known as Curral das Freiras (Valley of the Nuns). Between 1580 and 1640 Portugal and its islands were under Spanish rule and several new fortifications were constructed on Madeira, including the Fortaleza de São Tiago in the east of Funchal.

The English and Madeira

Following the marriage (in 1662) of Charles II of England and Catherine of Bragança (daughter of King João IV of Portugal) – a union in which Madeira narrowly escaped becoming part of the dowry – English involvement in the island increased. New commercial privileges were granted to English companies, in particular the right to export Madeiran wines to the New World.

As the production of sugar cane declined, due to competition from South American countries, more land was given over to vines. Throughout the 18th and 19th centuries many English, Irish and Scottish families settled in Madeira, and names such as Leacock, Cossart, Gordon and Blandy have since become synonymous with the history of Madeira and its wine.

As if to confirm this sentimental alliance, the British virtually occupied Madeira when they installed garrisons of troops on the island during the Napoleonic Wars. Twice in 1801, and again in 1807 for a seven-year period,

Vintage Madeira wine

Antique tiles depicting Madeiran life

several thousand soldiers were landed here to prevent any invasion by the French. Garrisoned in Monte, Camacha and Santo da Serra, they appear to have enjoyed their stay as they left a lasting genetic legacy in the form of fair hair and blue eyes, still found amongst the inhabitants of these areas.

During the 19th century Madeira's growing prosperity was stalled by a series of natural disasters. In 1803 floods swept through Funchal, destroying bridges and houses and killing around 600 of its citizens. Then cholera struck in 1852, carrying off some 7,000 victims. In the same year, and again in 1873, disease and insects devastated the island's vines. The Madeirans quickly responded to this series of potentially disastrous setbacks by constructing new channels for Funchal's rivers, stepping up the cultivation of bananas and crossing vines from America with local varieties to produce blight-resistant hybrids.

By the 1880s, Madeira had developed a reputation as a high-class tourist destination. Exiles, aristocrats, wintering Europeans and well-to-do invalids were all drawn to an island renowned for its mild, therapeutic climate. At first they stayed in the private country estates (called *quintas*) that Madeira's wealthy traders and landowners had built in the hills above Funchal. In time luxury hotels were established – most famously Reid's, which opened in 1891.

The port of Funchal

The 20th Century

In 1910, with the overthrow of the monarchy,
Portugal became a republic. Six years later the
country was dragged into the First World War
and Funchal was twice bombarded by German
submarines.

In the 1930s Portugal came under the
dictatorial rule of Dr António d'Oliveira Salazar;
his regime provoked a small uprising on the
island in 1931 – the only occasion in a long,
docile history that the Madeirans have barked
back at their compatriots on the mainland.
Their grievances arose from the introduction of
monopolistic laws that bankrupted two major
local banks, provoking a general strike and a
military coup that collapsed a few weeks later
when troops arrived from Lisbon.

During the Second World War Portugal
remained neutral, although Madeira did play
host to 2,000 British evacuees from Gibraltar.
The conflict brought a temporary halt to the
island's tourist trade, which slowly resumed in
the 1950s with visitors arriving by cruise ship
and seaplane. In 1960 an airport was built on
Porto Santo and four years later another
opened on Madeira. These developments
heralded a change in the type of tourist coming
to the island, as the leisured sea voyager who

might stay for a month was gradually replaced by the package holidaymaker jetting in for a week's winter sunshine.

On 25 April 1974 Portugal's popular revolution overthrew the government of Dr Marcello Caetano, a move welcomed by most Madeirans. Two years later the archipelago became an autonomous political region with its own government and parliament. Since then living standards on the island have steadily improved, with the Madeirans gaining further benefits from Portugal's entry into the European Community, which took place in 1986.

The People

Around 280,000 people live on Madeira, a third of them in the capital, Funchal, with some 5,000 on Porto Santo. Today's Madeirans are the descendants of settlers from all parts of Portugal, along with some Moorish and African influence from the days when slaves worked on the island.

Madeira has always been Roman Catholic, although several minority faiths now have churches on the islands. In the mid-16th century the islanders of Porto Santo gained some notoriety when a farmer and his niece declared themselves *profetas*, or prophets. Amongst their miraculous powers, they possessed the disquieting ability to itemise a person's past sins. The prophets quickly attracted a fanatical following, provoking so much consternation back in mainland Portugal that a magistrate was dispatched to arrest them. To this day the Porto Santo islanders are still sometimes referred to as *profetas*.

The islands' traditional sources of employment are agriculture, winemaking and fishing – and, in the last century, tourism. In the past, crop failure, market fluctuations and punitive taxation have forced many Madeirans to seek their fortunes elsewhere, and even today emigration and lengthy or regular periods of work abroad are a familiar fact of life. While early emigrants favoured Brazil and the Portuguese African colonies, popular destinations this century have been Venezuela, Curução and South Africa.

Today there are Madeirans working all over
the world, particularly in the oil industry and as
hotel and restaurant workers. The money they
send back to the island is an important factor in
the Madeiran economy, and every Christmas
planeloads of distant relatives pay an emotional
return visit to their tiny island. Some successful
emigrants later invest in their homeland – a
famous example is Manuel Pestana, the boy
from Ribeira Brava who went to South Africa in
the 1940s and made enough money to build
the Madeira Sheraton Hotel (now called the
Madeira Carlton).

Island Culture

The Madeirans are by nature calm and
conservative, and their destiny has largely
been determined by wealthy landowners and
foreign entrepreneurs. In the countryside the
islanders' patience and resilience is self-
evident in the carefully tended fields. Besides
the farmers working their terraces, you may
catch a glimpse of the cottage industries that
help supplement their income – the men
cultivating and working wicker, the women and
young girls embroidering cloth. Most rural
houses in Madeira are small, the mild weather
enabling their owners to spend much of the
day outdoors. In some villages the roadside is
more like an extended living room where
families congregate to sit and chat.

*Weaving a wicker
chair*

Many of the cultural characteristics found in
mainland Portugal are also present here, such
as unswerving faith in the family, the special
relationship with the British, a weakness for
bureaucracy and pomp and a passion for
festivals and folklore. At the same time the
Madeirans have forged an identity of their own
– this is an island of rugged *espada* fishermen,
of *espetada* (the local version of kebabs)
perfectionists, where the locals have an
inventive talent for making cakes and wine and
for wrapping trees with an assortment of
coloured light bulbs.

Here you can listen to both the laments of
Portuguese *fado* and to the islanders' own folk
songs; these are sometimes accompanied by
traditional instruments, such as the four-string
braguinha and the percussive *brinquinho* – a

hand-held pole where dolls wearing bells and castanets slide up and down to the music. Folk dances often hark back to the days of slavery – in the Ponta do Sol, dancers with bowed heads move in circles as if their feet were chained together.

Traditional Dress

Madeiran traditional dress, still regularly worn by flower-sellers, is smart and colourful. The women wear a red woollen skirt decorated with green, blue and yellow stripes, along with an embroidered red waistcoat over a white blouse. The men sport a baggy white shirt and knee-length trousers tied with a red sash. A *carapuça*, like a skull-cap with a stalk, and a *capa*, or cape, thrown over the shoulder, may also be worn, along with *botas*, light-coloured leather boots with a red stripe. The advent of tourism has encouraged a revival, at times rather contrived, of Madeiran traditions. Folk songs and dances are now a regular feature of hotel entertainment, and celebrations attractive to tourists have been added to the island's already busy calendar of religious festivals. Tourism is now vital to the island's economy but, with only one sandy beach and a history of high-class hospitality, the islands have escaped the bruising meeted out by package-tour travellers to more downmarket resorts. With new roads, a second golf course and two new 5-star hotels currently under construction, Madeira clearly intends to remain a premier holiday destination.

Dancing in traditional Madeiran dress

What to See

The essential rating system:

✓	'top ten'

♦♦♦   do not miss
♦♦   see if you can
♦   worth seeing if you
       have time

As most of the island's hotels are located in Funchal, many first-time visitors are given the impression that the majority of Madeira's sights can be found in and around the capital. This is slightly misleading, for while you can happily spend two or three days sightseeing in Funchal, you will not have seen Madeira until you have made a foray into the island's interior.

It is the landscape of Madeira, with its mountain peaks, terracing and abundant flora, that really impresses. If you only have time for one such trip, take the relatively short excursion to Curral das Freiras. For something more adventurous, pay a visit to the west of the island, in particular Paúl da Serra, Porto Moniz, São Vicente and the Boca da Encumeada. If you like mountains, head for the centre and the two peaks of Pico do Arieiro and Pico Ruivo. If you prefer to relax, consider taking the ferry or plane over to Porto Santo for a couple of nights. There is nothing there except a long, unspoilt beach and a sleepy way of life.

Câmara de Lobos

Touring by Car

While buses, taxis and coach tours are a viable way of seeing the island, a car allows you to explore and enjoy Madeira at your own pace – particularly if you stop overnight in one of the island's two *pousadas* (rural inns) or one of the hotels on the north coast.

Driving on Madeira can be tiring because, although the distances look short on a map, many of the roads consist of nothing but twists and turns, with a variety of bizarre hazards and weather conditions thrown in for good measure. Most visitors inevitably try to do too much in a day. Bear in mind that Madeira is covered with picnic sites and footpaths, and it is just as rewarding to aim for these as it is to hare around the island's churches, viewpoints and picturesque villages. For an easy day-trip by car from Funchal, try a visit to Curral das Freiras, Pico do Arieiro, Santana or Ponta de São Lourenço.

Levadas

Levadas (irrigation channels) are the icing on an already

WHAT TO SEE

satisfying cake. Soon after colonisation began, the Madeirans started constructing an elaborate system of watercourses to supply their crops. By the start of this century there were around 200 *levadas* on the island, which the Portugese government has now organised into an efficient network that waters the fields and provides hydro-electricity. As a result many of the channels have been repaired and concreted, with maintenance footpaths built beside them that make for easy walking. These are virtually level, and the flow of cool water alongside makes a pleasant companion. Follow a *levada* and it will lead you into the heart of Madeira, through the mountains to woods and valleys that restore meaning to those overworked words, peace and quiet. Some preliminary planning and preparation is advisable. If *levadas* flowed in circles Madeira really would be heaven, but for the moment you have the problem of getting to and from your starting and finishing points – often some considerable distance apart. Buses, taxis, organised excursions and willing co-drivers are all possible solutions, and many *levadas* reward a simple there-and-back walk.

Levadas can also be dangerous. They were not designed as public footpaths and they have few signposts. Sometimes they pass through long dark tunnels and sometimes there is no fence between you and a sheer drop to the valley floor. Waterfalls, landslides, mud, mist and rainstorms can make them unsafe, and you should not undertake a *levada* walk without suitable clothing and equipment. None of this should deter you, though. If you like walking and the peace of nature, then go with the flow. For guidance and inspiration, you will need a copy of the only book available on *levada* walking, *Landscapes of Madeira* by John and Pat Underwood (Sunflower Books), which can be bought on the island.

A typical levada

FUNCHAL

History

In the 1420s a Portuguese settlement was founded near to where Funchal's market now stands, its name inspired by the wild fennel (*funcho*) that grew on the surrounding plain. It was a natural choice for João Gonçalves Zarco, its first governor, because of the wide bay spanning out on either side and an amphitheatre of mountains behind to offer shelter from the northeasterly winds. Three rivers, now diverted into concrete channels disguised by bougainvillea, flowed towards the sea: the Ribeira de São João (which goes under the Rotunda do Infante), the Ribeira de Santa Luzia (now running alongside Rua 31de Janeiro) and Ribeira de João Gomes (alongside Rua de Dr Manuel Pestana Júnior). Despite their present forlorn and parched appearance, the waters from these rivers caused severe flood damage to the emerging city.

During the 16th century, town walls were built around Funchal as a response to frequent attacks from pirates. These were pulled down in the 1750s leaving only isolated forts – such as the inland Fortaleza do Pico, the Palácio de São Lourenço on the waterfront and the Fortaleza de São Tiago in the east. The modern development of the city followed the building of a new harbour breakwater out to the Loo Rock (hitherto a fortified island) in 1895, extended further in the 1930s. By the 1960s eight liners a day were calling here *en route* for Africa, Australia, the Caribbean and Latin America. As increasing numbers of visitors came to the island, new hotels were built in the west of the city. Between this hotel zone and the Old Town, which marks the eastern end of the city, lie most of the sights of ancient and modern Funchal.

Getting Around

Madeirans frequently bemoan the traffic congestion in their capital, but it is hardly worse than that found in many European cities. Funchal's one-way system scores better, and seems well designed to baffle and frustrate the uninitiated. Drivers should quickly try to befriend the city's principal east-west arteries – Estrada Conde de Carvalhal and Avenida do Infante.

Better still, do not bother with a car at all. You will need to take a bus (Nos 29, 30 or 31) or a taxi to get to the Jardim Botânico, but all the other sights listed below are within walking distance of Funchal's central landmark, the statue of Zarco in Avenida Arriaga. Some hotels provide courtesy buses from the hotel zone into the city centre; these usually stop on the south side of the Palácio de São Lourenço on the waterfront. Taxis are a convenient alternative – a cross-town journey only costs around 500 escudos. The Praça do Município is a welcoming place to be dropped, and for convenience, there is a taxi rank here when you need to return to your hotel.

◆◆◆
ADEGAS DE SÃO FRANCISCO ✓
(São Francisco Wine Lodges)

Avenida Arriaga 28

For a succinct, comprehensive and unpressured introduction to Madeira wine, take a guided tour round the best-known wine lodge on Madeira. Once part of Funchal's Franciscan monastery, the dark, vat-filled rooms of the lodge provide a pungent intitiation into the arcane processes required to make a bottle of Madeira. If you ever wanted to buy a bottle of 1863 Blandy's Boal (only 51,000 escudos), watch coopers working inside their massive oak barrels or just give an appreciative slap to a mahogany vat containing 11,440 gallons (52,000 litres) of this divine wine, this is the place. A

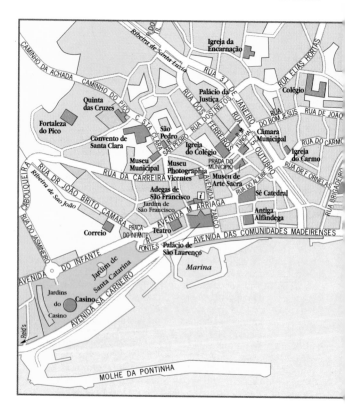

small historical museum displays wine-making memorabilia including antique tools, 18th-century accounts ledgers and the goatskin wine-bags (called *borrachos*) once used by the *borracheiros* who carried the wine down from the mountains. Tours last an hour and conclude with a free tasting.

Open: Monday–Friday 09.00–13.00 and 14.30–18.00 hrs, Saturday 09.00–13.00hrs. Guided tours Monday to Friday at 10.30 and 15.30hrs.

♦♦
AVENIDA DAS COMUNIDADES MADEIRENSES

Don't let the traffic racing along Avenida das Comunidades Madeirenses (formerly called Avenida do Mar) deter you from a walk along Funchal's seafront. On the south side of this road a long promenade stretches around the bay – a popular place to stroll in the early evening, when the city relaxes and workers drift down to the bars near the marina. At the western end of Funchal Bay is the Molhe da Pontina, where cruise ships visiting the capital moor up. It now incorporates a stub of rock where there used to be a 17th-century fortress, Nossa Senhora da Conceição, that protected the harbour. In the centre of the promenade is Funchal's new yacht marina, where boats can stop over before sailing across to the Caribbean. Its eastern side is bordered by the older Cais (Quay) which juts far enough into the sea to provide superb views back inland. In this area there are gardens, cafés, floating restaurants and kiosks where you can book boat excursions and ferry crossings to Porto Santo. Opposite the Diamante restaurant is a curious circular jigsaw of stone blocks, the Pilar de Banger. This is all that remains of a watchtower built in 1798 as a lookout for approaching ships. If you continue walking east you will cross the mouths of two of the rivers that run through the city, discover the unsightly chaos of the so called bus station (actually a car park), and eventually reach the Old Town. On the north side of Avenida das Comunidades Madeirenses, opposite the marina, you will see the cream and grey walls and watchtowers of the Palácio de São Lourenço. Considerably altered since its construction in the early 16th century, this fortress has ancient cannons poking through its battlements and sword-bearing soldiers guard the main gate in Avenida do Zarco. It is still in military hands and closed to the public, but you can visit its small museum on the Averida Arriaga side, opposite the tourist office. One block to the east is the 16th-century Alfândega (Customs House), now the seat of the islands' regional parliament. The circular modern building appended to one side is the debating chamber – the architectural merit of the building has itself long been a matter of debate.

◆

INSTITUTO DE BORDADOS, TAPEÇARIA E ARTESANATO DE MADEIRA
(Institute Of Madeiran Embroidery, Tapestry and Handicrafts)
Rua do Visconde de Anadia 44
A quiet museum devoted to Madeiran crafts, past and present, IBTAM is worth a visit if only to pay your respects to an enormous tapestry hanging in its entrance hall. The *Allegory of Madeira* took 14 girls three years to produce and contains an estimated 7 million stitches. Upstairs you can see traditional Madeiran costumes and musical instruments like the *brinquinho*, displays of historical embroidery tools and patterns, and more recent examples of marquetry, model-making and weaving.
Open: Monday–Friday 09.00–12.30 and 14.00–17.30hrs.

◆◆◆

JARDIM BOTÂNICO (Botanical Gardens)
Caminho do Meio
Funchal's Botanical Gardens were once a private estate, the Quinta do Bom Successo, owned by the Reid family (of Reid's Hotel – see page 32). Since 1960 it has been open to the public and contains a rich collection of plants and trees spread over terraces rising to 1,000ft (305m) above sea-level. Besides being a botanist's paradise, the gardens offer extensive views over Funchal and are a relaxing and accessible refuge from its urban bustle. Be sure to take some of the local *bolo de mel* fruit cake and all your unwritten postcards.
Open: daily 09.00–18.00hrs.

Nearby
Within the botanical gardens is a tiny **Museu de História Natural** (Natural History Museum). *Open*: daily 09.00–12.30 and 13.30–17.30hrs.
Next door on its southern corner is an exotic bird park, the **Jardim dos Loiros**. *Open*: daily 09.00–18.00hrs.
Orchid lovers should visit the nearby **Jardim Orquídea**, Rua Pita da Silva 37, where you can see how the flowers are

The Jardim Botânico

cultivated from seed.
Open: daily 09.00–18.00hrs.
Further south, below the
Estrada da Boa Nova, there are
orchids and other exotic
flowers on display and for sale
at **Quinta da Boa Vista**, Rua
Luis Figueiroa Albuquerque.
Open: Monday–Saturday
09.00–17.30hrs

◆
JARDIM DE SANTA CATARINA
Avenida do Infante
The Santa Catarina Garden is
an extensive public park
overlooking the harbour, just
west of the city centre. On its
eastern corner is the Rotunda
do Infante, where a statue of
Prince Henry the Navigator
stares coldly at the traffic
whizzing past his feet. Inside
the park another statue pays
homage to Christopher
Columbus, with the 17th-
century Capela de Santa
Catarina close by. A chapel has

stood here since 1425, the
original built by Zarco's wife,
Constança Rodriguez.
At the western end of the park
is a pink and white mansion,
Quinta Vigia, where the
president of Madeira's regional
government resides (gardens
open to the public). On the
opposite side of Avenida do
Infante is the grand Hospício da
Princesa, built in 1862 as a
tuberculosis sanatorium. To the
north you can see the Fortaleza
do Pico, constructed when the
island was under Spanish rule
and now used by the
Portuguese navy.

◆
JARDIM DE SÃO FRANCISCO
Avenida Arriaga
Close to the tourist office, this
municipal garden is shaded by
magnificent trees and is a useful
spot for catching your breath

while walking round the city. There is a small café and amphitheatre. Once part of the city's Franciscan monastery, the gardens now have a Scottish Kirk on their western side, founded in 1895.

Open: Tuesday–Friday 09.30–12.30 and 14.00–16.00hrs and during services.

On the south side of Avenida Arriaga is the Teatro Municipal and next door the city's former Associação Commercial e Industrial (Chamber of Commerce) – now, and perhaps aptly, a Toyota car showroom. Its walls are decorated with romantic *azulejos* (painted tiles) depicting scenes from Madeiran life.

If you walk east along Avenida Arriaga you will find a statue of the city's founder, João Gonçalves Zarco, which was erected in 1927. He is rather upstaged by the pompous façade of the Banco de

In Funchal's market

Portugal, which has an elegant interior that harmoniously unites *azulejos* and computer terminals.

◆◆◆
MERCADO DOS LAVRADORES (Workers' Market)
Rua Dr Fernão Ornelas
Despite the advent of supermarkets and shopping complexes, Funchal's market remains a focal point of city life and is well worth visiting both for its human comedy and the copious displays of local flowers, fruit and vegetables. Built in 1941, its entrance is heralded by flower-sellers wearing traditional Madeiran dress, while the ground and first floors are given over to stalls selling exotic fruits, vegetables, groceries and household items. Be sure to push on through to the fish hall to see its stone slabs draped with fierce-toothed *espada* and gory chunks of tuna.

Open: Monday–Thursday 07.00–16.00hrs, Friday 07.00–20.00hrs, Saturday 07.00–14.00hrs.

◆◆◆
MUSEU DE ARTE SACRA (Museum of Sacred Art)
Rua do Bispo 21
Housed in what was formerly the bishop's palace, this collection of religious treasures lies on the south side of Praça do Município. It is also the principal art museum of the islands, with the ground floor given over to impressive 15th and 16th-century Flemish paintings acquired as a result of Madeira's profitable sugar

trade with northern Europe. The first floor is occupied by displays of religious sculptures, liturgical vestments and ceremonial gold and silverware ranging in date from the 16th to the 20th century. While some of the best acquisitions are sometimes on loan elsewhere, there remains plenty to see and think about. Most of the exhibits come from the cathedral, from the Colégio church and from various convents and parish churches around Madeira. Together they are a telling reminder of the wealth and power the church enjoyed in these simple islands during previous centuries.
Open: Tuesday–Saturday 10.00–12.30 and 14.30–17.30hrs; Sunday 10.00–13.00hrs. *Closed*: the museum is expected to close for extensive renovation in the near future.

◆◆◆
MUSEU MUNICIPAL
Rua da Mouraria 31
There is no shortage of good reasons for visiting Funchal's delightful Municipal Museum, not least the fact that it stays open through the lunch hour. It is also thoroughly old-fashioned, built on the ennobling philosophy that so long as God's creatures are displayed in glass cabinets with clear labels the visitor's intellect can do the rest. You will find no audio-visual gadgetry here, just some revolving wooden doors that lead to a small dark aquarium where the walls swim with swivel-eyed groupers and disdainful triggerfish. Upstairs,

arranged like a military parade, are rows of stuffed fish, birds and insects from the Madeiran archipelago – part of a collection begun in 1850 and originally housed in the Palácio de São Lourenço.
Open: Tuesday–Friday 10.00–18.00hrs, Saturday and Sunday 12.00–18.00hrs.

◆◆
MUSEU PHOTOGRAPHIA VICENTES
Rua da Carreira 43
In 1865 Vicente Gomes da Silva set up a photographic studio in Funchal, the first in Portugal. From then until 1972, he and his descendants ran a photographic business from these premises in Rua da Carreira, amassing a collection of some 380,000 negatives that now form an invaluable documentary record of life on Madeira spanning more than a century. In 1978 the studio and its contents were taken over by the state, and many of its original props, furnishings and pieces of photographic equipment have survived. The negatives are still being catalogued, but a small and engrossing museum displaying some of the Vicentes' work has been opened above the Pátio. This courtyard can be entered from Rua da Carreira or Avenida do Zarco, and has a splendid curved balcony that evokes the atmosphere of old Funchal. A café, banana plants and the English Bookshop make the Pátio a charming place to take a break from sightseeing.
Open: Monday–Friday 14.00–18.00hrs.

FUNCHAL

◆◆◆
PRAÇA DO MUNICÍPIO ✓

Funchal's main square is a homage to monochrome. Paved with decorous curves of black and white stones, and bordered by whitewashed buildings outlined in dark basalt, it is an attractive place to sit and watch the world go by. From its central fountain you can see the hills rising beyond the city.

On the north side of the square is the Baroque Igreja do Colégio, with the former Jesuit College beside it. The Jesuits arrived in Madeira in 1569, erecting a church, college and monastery which they occupied until their expulsion from Portugal in 1760. The college, at one time used to billet British troops, is now part of Funchal's university. The church was completed in 1641 and has an imposing, time-stained facade including four marble statues of saints with, if you're lucky, a pigeon on each head. In contrast to its external austerity, the interior is zealously decorated and every surface is either painted or tiled with *azulejos*. *Open*: daily 17.00–18.00hrs and during services.

On the south side is the former Bishop's Palace, built in 1750, which now houses the Museu de Arte Sacra (see page 28).

On the east side is the harmonious late 18th-century Câmara Municipal (Town Hall), once the private residence of the Conde de Carvalhal, one of Madeira's wealthiest landowners. Inside there is an inner courtyard with a fountain and *azulejos* (decorated tiles), and upstairs the Museu da Cidade. This records the evolution of Funchal through the centuries, culminating in the visit of Pope John Paul II to Madeira in 1991. The displays include early maps of the city, models of Funchal's fortresses, romantic 19th-century prints of Madeira and photographs of the bomb damage incurred during the First World War. *Open*: Monday–Friday 09.00–12.30 and 14.00–17.00hrs.

◆◆◆
QUINTA DAS CRUZES
Calçada do Pico 1

Walk uphill from the São Pedro church (Calçada de Santa Clara) and you will reach the pink walls of the Quinta das Cruzes. Once aloof from the town, this estate has been engulfed by a modern city but still remains tranquil. Here you can get a glimpse of the luxurious lifestyle enjoyed by the island's wealthy residents, and appreciate how, in Madeira, a garden is given as much status and attention as the house it surrounds.

Once owned by a wine-shipping family, the mansion dates back to the 17th century and contains a wide-ranging collection of period furniture, antiques, porcelain and furnishings. Spread over 16 rooms, it includes many *objets d'art* from around the world including English furniture, porcelain from the East India Company and treasures from Portugal's colonies. Exhibits of local interest include a litter used to carry passengers around the island, furniture recycled from the cases made for exporting sugar and the finds from a Dutch galleon shipwrecked off Porto Santo in 1724.

In the grounds of the *quinta* there are many fine trees and flowers and an archaeological park dotted with ivy-clad tombstones, sculptures, coats-of-arms and two window frames, dating to 1577, decorated in the Manueline style with seafaring motifs. *Open*: Tuesday–Sunday 10.00–12.30 and 14.00–18.00hrs. The gardens remain open through the lunch break.

Nearby

Next door to the Quinta das Cruzes is the **Convento de Santa Clara**. Although the present convent dates from the 17th century, there has been a building on this site since the 15th century – it was from here that nuns fled to Curral das Freiras (see page 42) to escape an attack on the city by pirates in 1566. The adjacent church is richly decorated with blue, yellow and white *azulejos* tiles and the tomb of the islands' discoverer, João Gonçalves Zarco, lies beneath the altar. *Open*: knock to gain admission.

Funchal's main square, the Praça do Município

REID'S HOTEL

One of the world's great hotels, Reid's rises commandingly above the cliffs overlooking Funchal harbour. It presents its best façade to the sea, from where most of its famous and wealthy guests have arrived since its opening in 1891. The hotel was founded by a Scotsman, William Reid who, at the age of 14, left the family farm in Kilmarnock to seek his fortune. Working his passage to Lisbon and Funchal, he found employment in the wine trade, eventually making enough money to start a business letting *quintas* (estates) to the island's aristocratic visitors.

Built by the same architects who designed the Shepheard's Hotel in Cairo, Reid's is now owned by the Blandy family. Despite the addition of new accommodation wings, it remains a discreet and luxurious sanctuary with an atmosphere hovering between English country house and colonial club. The hotel still attracts the famous and the titled, and boasts an illustrious guest book with autographs ranging from George Bernard Shaw and Winston Churchill to Gregory Peck.

For many visitors to Madeira, afternoon tea on the terrace at Reid's is as essential as a ride on the Monte toboggans. Some settle into a wicker armchair and contemplate the cruise ships below, while others sit in the lounge with a copy of yesterday's *Times*. Tea arrives with crustless sandwiches and Madeira cake and the days of civility and ritual are fondly remembered. If this all sounds too staged, the poolside buffet lunch is good value, or you can pop in to the Cocktail Bar one evening (suit and tie requested). What to drink? Why, vintage Madeira, m'dear.

SÉ (Cathedral)
Rua do Aljube

At the end of the 15th century two architects, Gil Eanes and Pero Annes, were sent from the Portuguese mainland to organise the construction of Funchal's cathedral. Work began in 1485 using the local basalt stone and the building was completed 29 years later. Above the main entrance you can see the Portuguese royal coat of arms. The interior is rather dark, but it is still possible to appreciate the Moorish-style ceiling carved from Madeiran wood and inlaid with ivory.

ZONA VELHA (Old Town)

Funchal's Old Town lies to the east of the bus station and market, and is marked by a small sign: *Zona Velha da Cidade*. Traditionally the fishermen's quarter, it has so far escaped gentrification and remains an easy-going muddle of small workshops, boatyards and fish restaurants. Walking east along Rua de Carlos I, you reach a pedestrianised precinct of cobbled streets and the simple 16th-century Capela do Corpo Santo. At the end of the street is the cream and brown Fortaleza de São Tiago, which dates from 1614 and which was still used by the Portuguese

military until recently. Now it is closed but there are plans to use it to house a Museum of Modern Art. Rua do Portão de São Tiago, a small lane, leads behind it, passing through an area of run-down houses to the elegant 18th-century Igreja de Santa Maria Maior. This seaside church is also known as the Igreja do Socorro (Church of Salvation) in commemoration of the help given by São Tiago (St James) during an epidemic in the 16th century. If you look east along the coast you can just see the statue of Christ at Ponta da Garajau, and beyond it the Ilhas Desertas. The beach here, Praia de Barreirinha, is currently being developed and will eventually be turned into a new lido complex.

Funchal's cathedral, built of basalt in 1485

PRACTICAL FUNCHAL

Accommodation

Virtually all of the hotels in Funchal are located in the west of the city. Four of the island's six luxurious 5-star hotels are grouped conveniently close to each other around the western end of Avenida do Infante, with another 20 hotels in the 3 and 4-star categories spread along the Estrada Monumental. This hotel zone is located only a short ride by taxi or bus from the city centre. It has its own restaurants and shopping centres, with good public swimming pools at the Lido in Rua Gorgulho.

Luxury Hotels
Casino Park, Quinta da Vigia (tel: 233111).
Designed in the 1970s by the Brazilian architect Oscar Niemeyer, this is a long curved 400-room block set on the cliffs overlooking the harbour. The grounds include a casino, cinema and conference centre.
Madeira Carlton, Largo António Nobre (tel: 231031).
Formerly part of the Sheraton group, this modern 375-room hotel is spread over 18 floors. There are four restaurants and a good range of entertainment and sports facilities including swimming in two pools and the sea.
Reid's, Estrada Monumental (tel: 766466).
Madeira's most famous hotel has now been pampering

Guests enjoying the pool at Madeira's Savoy hotel

guests for over a century. With over 300 staff, mature gardens (only open to residents), restaurants to suit all moods, extensive sports facilities and high-class organised excursions, its popularity is unlikely to wane.
Savoy, Avenida do Infante (tel: 222031).
Established in 1912 but completely rebuilt in the 1960s, the Savoy has earned a reputation for quality, comfort and service. There are 350 rooms, spacious lounges, secluded gardens, shops and a nightclub.

Three and Four-Star Hotels
Eden Mar, Rua do Gorgulho (tel: 762221).

Spacious suite hotel close to the sea, the shops and the Lido complex. All rooms have a kitchenette and balcony.
Estrelícia, Camino Velha da Ajuda (tel: 230131).
Part of a high-rise complex that includes the apartment-hotels Mimosa and Buganvília. The atmosphere is relaxed and functional, with two swimming pools and a weekly entertainment programme.
Monte Carlo, Calçada da Saúde 10 (tel: 226131).
Once a private residence, this is a modest yet attractive 3-star hotel set on a steep hill just north of Quinta das Cruzes. There are 45 rooms of varying size, a terrace with views and a restaurant.
Windsor, Rua das Hortas 4 (tel: 233081).
This busy but friendly 4-star hotel is located right in the city centre with a small restaurant and rooftop swimming pool.

Pensions
Astória, Rua João Gago 10 (tel: 223820).
A modest two-star *pensão* near the cathedral.
Mónaco, Rua das Hortas 14 (tel: 230191).
A comfortable 3-star *residêncial* (small hotel) in the centre of Funchal.
Quinta da Penha de Franca, Rua Penha de Franca 2 (tel: 229080).
Officially a 4-star *albergaria*, this is a small homely hotel with a pool and garden. Close to the Savoy Hotel, it incorporates Joe's Snack Bar and there are many more good restaurants nearby.

Restaurants
Hotel Zone
Madeira's 5-star hotels have some of the finest restaurants in Portugal. At Reid's, **Les Faunes** offers gourmet-standard French cuisine amidst a cool blue décor and Picasso lithographs; alternatively you can enjoy the marble columns and chandeliers of the **Main Dining Room** (evenings only), which has reasonably priced set menus. The Savoy's **Fleur-de-Lys Grill Room** is equally prestigious, with panoramic views of Funchal at night, while the **O Churrasco Grill** at the Madeira Carlton serves Portuguese specialities in a cosy, candlelit ambience.
All these are smart and expensive, but you can dine equally well in the smaller restaurants that have gathered at the feet of these great hotels. Walk down Rua Imperatriz Dona Amélia, behind the Savoy,and you can take your pick of international cuisines and accompanying musicians. One of the best is **Casa Velha** (tel: 225749) at No 69, a restored 19th-century house with a warm atmosphere, interesting menus and friendly service. Here too you will find the pricey **Dona Amélia** at No 83 (tel: 225784) or the popular **Casa dos Reis** (tel: 225182) in the adjacent Rua de Penha Franca.
For a leisurely lunch, the **Escola de Hotelaria e Turismo** at Quinta Magnólia (Rua do Dr Pita) offers good food made and served with great seriousness by the students of Madeira's Hotel School. Formerly the

British Country Club, the *quinta* has pleasant grounds with a swimming pool, tennis courts and children's play area. A four-course lunch is served with a choice of set dishes in the restored main building, which also has a terrace where you can take tea from 16.00 to 19.00hrs with home-made cakes. Tables for lunch must be booked at least a day in advance (tel: 764013, closed Sundays).

City Centre
Walk along Rua da Carreira around 13.00hrs on a weekday and you can enjoy the buzz of the city at lunchtime. This street has several unpretentious and moderately priced restaurants – such as **Dragão Vermelha** (No 54), **Londres** (No 64), **O Funil** (No 132) and, one of the best, **Fim de Século** (No 144; tel: 224476).

For something more lavish, try **O Celeiro**, Rua dos Aranhas 22 (tel: 230622) opposite the Centro Commercial Infante. For something simple, pop into **Pastelaria Rosa Vermelha**, Rua dos Netos 39.

If it is sunny and you prefer to stay outside, take a snack to one of Funchal's splendid gardens, such as the Jardim de São Francisco or the one at Quinta das Cruzes.

For an evening meal, there are several floating restaurants along the seafront of which the largest and most covetable is **The Vagrant** (tel: 223572). Also known as 'The Beatles' Boat', it was once owned by the pop group – fortunately customers dining within its polished wood

A tempting display of freshly cooked seafood

and tinted glass are spared endless piped renditions of *Let it Be*. In the Old Town, two restaurants specialising in fish and seafood are both situated close to the Capela do Corpo Santo. The **Golfinho**, Largo do Corpo Santo 21 (tel: 226774), has an impressive nautical decor with portholes, navigational instruments and walls faced with wood and brass. The **Estrela do Mar**, Largo do Corpo Santo 1-7 (tel: 228255) is more expensive but it also has more inventive dishes on its menu, with a good line in flamboyant *flambés*.

Shopping

Antiques There are several antique and second-hand shops in the streets adjacent to the São Pedro church (Rua São Pedro), and a bric-a-brac shop at Rua da Carriera 85.

Clothes Traditional Madeiran leather boots and tyre-soled shoes can be bought direct from a small workshop in the Old Town at Gonçalves & Sousa, Rua do Portão de São Tiago 22. For cheap modern shoes try the *sapatarias* in Rua da Boa Viagem and other streets near the Mercado dos Lavradores. If you fancy a hat as modelled by the old men of Madeira, visit Salão Londrino, Rua dos Ferreiros 128.

Embroidery Patricio & Gouveia, Rua do Visconde de Anadia 33, has spacious showrooms selling Madeiran *bordados* and offers visitors an open invitation to see the pattern-printing and finishing processes that take place on the premises. Other quality shops include Madeira Sun, Avenida do Infante 26B, and Imperial, Rua do Castanheiro 26. For needlework rugs, hangings and kits visit Maria Kiekeben at Rua da Carreira 194.

Food The combined shop and café called A Lua, Rua da Carriera 78, sells a good range of bread and cakes – including its own *bolo de mel* (fruit cake). Rua Dr Fernão Ornelas has a few old-fashioned delicatessens, with the Mercado dos Lavradores at its

Pavement restaurants lining the streets of the Old Town

eastern end. In the hotel zone, the Lido Sol shopping centre, Estrada Monumental 318, has a large supermarket (*open*: daily 09.00–21.00hrs).

Flowers There are flower-sellers outside the cathedral and the Mercado dos Lavradores. Many of the top hotels have florists in their lobby shops, and you can order flowers boxed for taking home from A Rosa Florista, Rua Imperiatriz D Amélia 126 (tel: 764111).

Jewellery Tavir, Rua de João Tavira 8, specialises in silver.

Leather Artecouro, Rua da Alfândega 15.

Souvenirs Just behind the Teatro Municipal, in Ruado Conselheiro José Silvestre Ribeiro, is 'The Famous Shop' (as it styles itself), Casa Turista.

Shopping in Funchal

A cross between a stately mansion and a department store, this is a souvenir shop *par excellence*. If you don't have time to visit the rest of the island in search of Madeiran crafts, it is all here. Besides a high-quality selection of Madeiran embroidery, ceramics, tapestries, wickerwork, knitted garments and wine, there is a small *palheiro* (thatch-roofed cottage), trellises of vines, banana and sugar cane plants and a selection of local flora. Staff speak English, French and German and can arrange for purchases to be shipped home.

Wicker Sousa & Gonçalves have a wicker warehouse at Rua do Castanheiro 47, and there is a small wicker shop at Rua da Carreira 102.

Wine For advice and a full list of the wine lodges and shops in Madeira you can visit the Instituto da Vinho da Madeira, Rua de Outubro 78. There is a small museum here but no wine for sale (*open*: Monday–Friday 09.30–12.00 and 14.00–17.00 hrs). Two old and pleasantly fusty lodges can be found in Rua dos Ferreiros: D'Oliveiras at No 107 and, further up the hill, Henriques & Henriques, with a vine-roofed courtyard, at No 125. Diogos Wine Shop, Avenida Arriaga 48, has a comprehensive selection of wines with a small, idiosyncratic museum downstairs dedicated to Columbus and to 19th-century tourism in Madeira (*open*: Monday–Friday 10.00–13.00 and 15.00–19.00 hrs; Saturday 10.00–13.00hrs).

Souvenirs with a nautical theme

Entertainment

The best shows in town are in the big hotels, with Madeiran folklore, *fado* and international floorshows frequently providing the inspiration for an evening out. **The Savoy** holds afternoon tea dances, jazz nights and, on Thursdays, a bridge tournament. The **Madeira Carlton** has classical concerts and cabarets while New York, Vienna and Paris are the themes of the **Casino Park's** regular dinner and show entertainments. In the same hotel you can visit the **Casino da Madeira** with roulette, blackjack and slot machines (you will need to take your passport). All these hotels have discos or nightclubs. If you prefer to join the locals, head for **Vespas** disco, Avenida Sá Carneiro (open: daily 23.00–04.00hrs).

AROUND FUNCHAL

A great variety of sights lie within easy reach of Funchal. These can be visited on a half-day trip, or combined to make an easy-going day. All feature in the organised excursions available from any hotel, and can be reached by bus or taxi.

◆◆
CÂMARA DE LOBOS

Madeira was once the home of large colonies of seals and the village of Câmara de Lobos, 5 miles (8km) west of Funchal, gets its name from the *lobos do mar* (sea-wolves) spotted here by the island's first settlers. Partly because it was a popular subject for the paintbrush of Sir Winston Churchill, who first visited the island in 1950, Câmara de Lobos is frequently portrayed as a quaint and picturesque fishing village. This is misleading: parts of the port are scruffy and poor and, despite bringing in much of the island's catch of *espada* fish, there is insufficient work for all its inhabitants. Even so, there are pretty spots where behatted old men continue to play cards on upturned boats as if the rest of the world did not exist.

If you are coming from Funchal along the EN101, you will see two roads leading to the port marked Cais (Quay) and Vila (Town). Take the second (after the Shell garage), which leads down to a small terrace with a bandstand. Here you will find a selection of fish restaurants and the restored 18th-century church of São Sebastião. If you walk toward the sea, there is a

clifftop path to the left which passes the tourist office to reach the fishing harbour. To return to the bandstand, turn left along Rua São João de Deus.

For a good view over the village you should visit the *miradouro,* or viewpoint, at Pico da Torre, which is easily reached by driving a short way out of Câmara de Lobos, in the direction of Ribiera Brava, and then turning right.

Restaurants

Riba-Mar, Largo da República (tel: 942113). A well-established family-run fish restaurant. There is an upstairs dining room with pleasant nautical décor and wooden floors, or tables and chairs outside. The menu offers a wide choice of fish and seafood at moderate to expensive prices.

A Praia (tel: 942354). Reached by some steps down from the

Gaily painted boats moored up on the unspoiled fishing beach at Câmara de Lobos

Largo da República, this is a casual, typically Madeiran fish restaurant close to the sea. Look for signs advertising the *prato do dia* (speciality of the day), such as *arroz de mariscos* (rice with shellfish) served in a large terracotta bowl. Reasonable prices.

◆◆◆
CURRAL DAS FREIRAS ✓

In 1566 the nuns of the Santa Clara convent in Funchal fled inland to escape from the pirates who were attacking the city. They sought refuge in the remote valley of the Ribeira das Socorridos, which subsequently became known as the Curral das Freiras (the Valley of the Nuns). At the time their journey across the mountains must have been a lengthy ordeal, but today their secret valley is just an 11½-mile (19-km) drive from Funchal. If you take the Rua Dr Pita out of Funchal, your trip could easily include a stop off at Pico dos Barcelos (see page 46). From here the EN105 and EN107 lead north, climbing steadily up to cool forests of eucalyptus and pine.

Be sure to take the short detour

The protective figure of the Virgin and Child

to Eira do Serrado (3,588 feet/1,094m), down a cobbled road to the right. A short walkway leads up to a *miradouro* (viewpoint) – one of the best on the island. From here, if the clouds are favourable, there are superb views over Curral das Freiras. This is a good place to pause and study the intensive terracing that has turned the valley walls into steep green staircases. You will also see a tiny road snaking down towards the village far below – your route into the valley. Until the end of the 1950s Curral das Freiras could only be reached by narrow mountain paths winding down to the valley floor – you can see remnants of them as you make your descent through tunnels to the isolated settlement that has grown up here. Today a new road is being built on the north side of the valley which will soon link it to Boaventura. For the moment, though, you must stop by the stream – a good point to sit and wonder what it must be like to live in this natural haven. If it is sunny and the scent of flowers is wafting your way, one name may well spring to mind: the legendary earthly paradise of Shangri-La.

Events
In early November a Festa da Castanha (Chestnut Festival) is held in the village.

◆
ILHAS DESERTAS
Just 10 miles (16km) southeast of Madeira, the Ilhas Desertas make a tantalising sight. Rising to 1,571ft (479m), they must

have provoked the imagination of the island's first settlers as much as they do visitors today. Despite repeated attempts down the centuries they have stubbornly resisted human colonisation and so far they only have one practical use – as a barometer. If you look to the horizon and the Desertas seem very near, say the islanders, then bad weather is imminent. Once privately owned by a British family, the Desertas now belong to the state. Even though they have little soil or fresh water, the islands have become a sanctuary for numerous seabirds, wild goats

Dawn comes up over the distant Ilhas Desertas

and a poisonous black spider, *Lycosa ingens*. Parts of the largest island, Deserta Grande, are a nature reserve policed by lonely biologists who watch over a small colony of monk seals.

If you are sufficiently intrigued, boat trips to the islands can be booked from Funchal's Marina, where companies like Turipesca (tel: 231063) and Costa do Sol (tel: 238538) organise boat excursions to various destinations along Madeira's south coast.

AROUND FUNCHAL

◆◆◆ MONTE ✓

Leafy and genteel, Monte is a reminder of the days when Madeira was an exclusively upper-class holiday resort. If you had come here a century ago, you would most likely have arrived by hammock or palanquin, or on the railway, opened in 1894, that once climbed up from Funchal to Terreiro da Luta (it closed in 1939 following a fatal boiler explosion). From the mid-19th century until the outbreak of the Second World War, this hilltop village was a distinguished health resort surrounded by *quintas* (estates), chapels and sanatoriums where the rich and ailing resided.

Today Monte's famous mountain air is as refreshing and therapeutic as ever, and its grassy cobblestones and neglected woods make it a pleasant place to stroll and picnic. In the main square, Largo da Fonte, there is a bandstand, a café and a shrine to the Virgin of Monte. A sloping bridge, which once carried the railway, stretches above the diligently maintained formal gardens, laid out in 1894. From the square you can climb some steps, or take the cobbled Camino das Babosas, to the church of Nossa Senhora do Monte, one of the most famous sights in Madeira. Our Lady of Monte is the patron saint of the Madeiran islands and on 14 and 15 August, the Feast of the Assumption, the church is the focus of an annual pilgrimage in her honour. For a few intense days Monte's tranquil streets are crowded with worshippers, some of whom climb on their knees up the long flight of steps in front of the church. Built in the late 18th century, the church contains a statue of the Virgin Mary found near Terreiro da Luta in the 15th century. To the left of the church is a side chapel where Charles I, the last Emperor of Austria and Hungary, is buried. Exiled after the First World War, he and his family came to Madeira in 1921, staying at Reid's and the Quinta Gordon in Monte. A year later the 35-year-old monarch died of pneumonia.

Open: daily 08.00–13.00hrs and during services.

If you continue along the Caminho das Babosas you will meet the Old Monte bar and the gardens of Quinta Nossa Senhora da Conceição, also known as the Old Monte Gardens. *Open:* Monday–Friday 10.00–18.00hrs.

The lane then curls round to the Largo das Babosas where there is a small chapel. A cobbled path nearby leads into the Ribeira de João Gomes valley. This continues round to Romeiros, from where there are walks east along the Levada dos Tornos and the Levada da Serra.

Toboggan Ride

Just below the steps of Monte's church is the starting point for the celebrated ride down to Funchal by *carro de cesto*. This is a form of public transport unique to Madeira, where one

Aboard the Monte Toboggan Ride – a must for every visitor

or two passengers can slide down to Funchal in what looks like a cross between a wicker sofa and a laundry basket set on wooden runners. The *carro de cesto* is similar to the sledges that were once used by Madeirans to slide agricultural produce down from the high terraces to the island's harbours, but here the descent is more dignified. Each toboggan is guided by two drivers dressed in white flannels, boaters and traditional leather boots. Together they push, pull and coax their human cargo down the steep cobbled slipways, at times gaining considerable (but not dangerous) speed.

For many visitors, particularly for cruise ship passengers with limited time, the Monte toboggan ride is the essential Madeiran experience and many find it exhilarating. A choice of two trips is offered along the same route: a short one of just over 1 mile (2km) from Monte to Livramento, and another that goes to within a five-minute walk of the city centre. This latter journey, which covers 2½ miles (4km) and takes about 20 minutes, costs around 2,200 escudos per person plus tip. In the past the drivers then had to carry their *carros de cesto* back up to Monte, but now they are simply loaded onto a lorry.

◆
PICO DOS BARCELOS
At 1,207ft (364m), this peak provides an excellent view over Funchal. Take the Rua Dr Pita north from the Hotel Zone,

bearing left along Caminho de Santo Martinho. This leads to the São Martinho church, which enjoys a dominant position overlooking the west of the city. Turn right here and you will reach Pico dos Barcelos.

Restaurant
The best way to enjoy this mountain peak is to have a drink or a meal in one of the restaurants nearby. The terrace of the **Bodião** (tel: 263078) offers splendid views across the valley to the mountains beyond. In the foreground is the church of São António, with its distinctive tiled steeples. The restaurant's menu is simple, with a selection of fish on display – including the delicious local *bodião* (parrot fish). Prices are reasonable and the service attentive.

◆◆
QUINTA DO PALHEIRO FERREIRO
Also known as Blandy's Gardens, this 800-acre (324-ha) country estate was first owned by the wealthy Madeiran landowner, the Conde de Carvalhal, who started planting out its impressive landscape gardens in the early 1800s. Since 1884 it has been owned by the Blandy family and they have created a horticultural wonderland of gracious lawns, aristocratic trees and gardens richly stocked with brilliantly coloured flowers. The *quinta* lies 5 miles (8km) east of Funchal. Leave via the Rua Dr Manuel Pestana Júnior, following the EN201-1 towards Camacha. Shortly after you pass the junction with the

EN102 to São Gonçalo there is a signposted turning to the right.
Open: Monday–Friday 09.30–12.30hrs.

TERREIRO DA LUTA

The largest monument in Madeira stands just over 1 mile (2km) north of Monte on the road to Camacha (the EN201). In the 15th century the statue of Nossa Senhora (Our Lady) of Monte was miraculously discovered near here by a shepherdess; the statue now stands on the altar of the church dedicated to her in Monte. In 1917, following the bombing of Funchal by German submarines, many Madeirans made a pilgrimage to Monte to pray for salvation. A vow was made that if peace came the islanders would erect another statue in honour of Our Lady of Monte. Ten years later this enormous statue at Terreiro da Luta (The Battlefield) was completed. It is 18ft (5.5m) high and weighs 20 tonnes. At the base is a rosary made from the anchor chains of a French ship torpedoed in Funchal Bay in 1916. Both the chains and the stones were carried up the mountain by the faithful.

Nature's profusion contrasts with strict geometry in one of Monte's gardens

MADEIRA: WEST

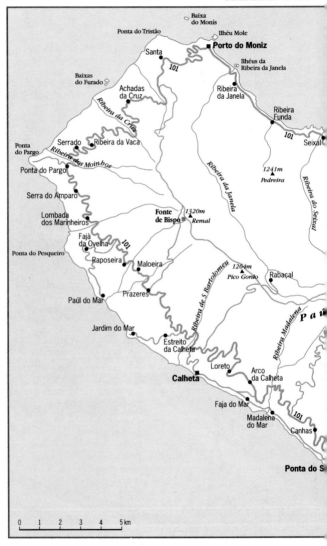

THE WEST

Go west and you will discover
the rich diversity of Madeira's
landscape. Here the Ribeira
Brava and Ribeira de São
Vicente have cut deep into the
island, forming two steep-sided
valleys, running north to south,
that virtually split the island in
two. Climb up to the plateau of
Paúl da Serra, which lies
beyond these valleys to the
west, and you will be surprised
to find that not only does
Madeira have lush, sub-tropical
vegetation, it also has airy
expanses of moorland too.
Drop down to the bleaker north
coast, hammered by the
prevailing northeasterly winds,
and you will find curtains of
sheer basalt cliffs down which
waterfalls plunge to the sea –
some times via the roof of your
motor car.
The south coast is more
populated and prosperous,with
a string of small villages
running along the hills and
valleys. Here you can enjoy the
classic postcard Madeira of
whitewashed churches and
houses garlanded with flowers
and vines, their terracotta roofs
warmed by the southern
Atlantic sun.

Getting Around

Most of western Madeira can
be seen by coach or minibus
excursions from Funchal. Their
normal route is via Ribeira
Brava and Paúl da Serra, with a
stop at Porto do Moniz for
lunch. The return journey
continues along the north coast
to São Vicente, then either
south via Boca de Encumeada to
Ribeira Brava or on to Santana

and Ribeiro Frio. A few take the less interesting south coast road via Calheta. Avoid trips that offer to show you the west in half a day – this will be exhausting and meaningless. If you are driving make an early start and try to visit Paúl da Serra in the morning, when there is less chance of finding it thick with cloud. Staying a night in Ribeira Brava, Porto do Moniz, São Vicente or at the Pousada dos Vinháticos will make the trip much more enjoyable.

Paúl da Serra can also be reached by a spectacular mountain road (the EN204), only recently completed, that runs west from Boca da Encumeada. If you decide to return to Funchal along the southern coastal road (the EN101), you can take the new fast road (the EN213) after

Calheta that runs along the seashore through a series of spectacular tunnels to Ribeira Brava.

◆
CALHETA
Follow the winding EN101 along the serried hills and valleys of the south coast and you will find some quintessential Madeiran countryside. Here the land seems effortlessly bountiful, with bananas, vines, vegetables and fruit trees flourishing in the fields, and the roadside awash with colourful flowers.

The villages of Arco da Calheta and Estreito da Calheta, and below them the port of Calheta, are typical of the seemingly idyllic lifestyle this sunny corner

High above the clouds on the mountains of western Madeira

Patchwork quilt terraces

of the island enjoys. As you drop down to Calheta you can see one of the steep cobbled alleys where produce from the terraced fields above was once slid down on wood and wicker toboggans to the harbour.

Many of the churches along this part of the coast date from the 16th and 17th centuries – Calheta's parish church was rebuilt in 1639 and has a carved wooden ceiling in the Moorish style. One of the finest Flemish paintings now hanging in Funchal's Museu de Arte Sacra, called the *Encontro de Santa Ana com São Joaquim (The Meeting Between St Anne and St Joachim)*, once hung in the village church at Madalena do Mar, 1.8 miles (3km) to the south.

Accommodation

Estalegem Conda Azul (tel: 823033). Opened in 1992, this is a clean rather isolated hotel right next to the sea. There are only 10 rooms, all on the first floor and with a balcony. A large restaurant below specialises in fish and seafood. A sailing marina is under construction nearby.

◆◆◆
PAÚL DA SERRA ✓

If you are coming from Ribeira Brava look for a turning right shortly after Canhas, where a road (the EN208) climbs up through well-cultivated terraces to cool forests fragrant with eucalyptus and pine. At some point you will probably pass through the clouds, emerging above the treeline in the sparse and exhilarating landscape of Paúl da Serra. The largest plateau on Madeira, this is a windswept and often misty area of open moorland where cattle and sheep graze. If the weather is good you will have stunning views out across the island. If it is bad you can try directing your complaints to the enormous white statue of Christ, the Nosso Senhor da Montanha, erected in 1962, which stands near the junction with the EN204. This is a fast, straight dorsal road that runs west towards Porto do Moniz from Bocada Encumeada. At Fonte de Bispo there is a *miradouro* (viewpoint) with good views over the green valley of Ribeira da Janela.

◆
PONTA DO SOL

As its name suggests, this is one of the sunniest points on the island, 5½ miles (9km) west of Ribeira Brava. Before the building of the new coastal road to Calheta, villages like this were only linked to the outside world by boat and an umbilical track leading to the high road (the EN101) above. Today Ponta do Sol is ripe for development, with palm trees, promenade cafés and a 1930s cinema (now home to the local police) creating an incipient Riviera atmosphere.

◆
PONTA DO PARGO

The western tip of Madeira is said to be called Dolphin Point because Zarco and his crew caught one of these *pargos* in the waters nearby – these are not the mammal dolphins,

Sunny Ponta do Sol

however, but the dolphin fish that sometimes features on Madeiran restaurant menus. The village stands high in the hills, but a road leads down to a lighthouse from where there are good views along the west coast. This blunt end of the island, between here and Achadas da Cruz, has a benign, Alpine feel that supports the description of Madeira as a sub-tropical Switzerland. It is as if a gardener had scattered a packet of 'Mixed Abundance' in the rich earth long ago, creating lush, shady forests where pines and sinewy eucalyptus mingle with rampaging hydrangeas and sedate pockets of maize, cabbages and apple trees.

Events
In September a Festa da Pêra (Pear Festival) is held at Ponta do Pargo.

THE WEST

◆◆
PORTO DO MONIZ

Porto do Moniz is a remote village on the north western tip of Madeira. A former whaling station, it is the furthest away from Funchal you can get and worth visiting purely for the satisfaction of the journey there. It has no 'sights' whatsoever, just a wild, sea-battered feel that tempts many to stay a night or two. There is an adequate range of restaurants and accommodation, and two safe seawater swimming pools that get busy in the summer.

For a good overview of Porto do Moniz, take the serpentine road up towards Santa. Looking down, you can see the patchwork of bracken-fenced plots where the villagers grow vegetables and fruit. Off shore lies the Ilhéu Mole with its lighthouse.

Events

An agricultural festival and cattle show takes place near here in July.

Accommodation

Residêncial Calhau (tel: 852104). A peaceful, 15-room pension perched on the rocks, with dark wooden furniture and colourful woven rugs used as curtains, bedspreads and rugs. All rooms have balconies overlooking the sea and the nearby swimming pool.

Residêncial Orca, Sítio das Pagos (tel: 852359). Right next door to the Calhau, and with similar sea views, the 12-room Orca has a lounge and large restaurant.

Parque de Campismo (tel: 852447). A modest camp site.

Restaurants

Cachalote (tel: 852180). Looking like an ice-box washed up on the rocks, this is the best place to eat in Porto do Moniz. There are two dining rooms, one with a cane ceiling and wood floor, another above with modern white furniture. Both have good seaviews and the restaurant can get busy with coach parties at lunchtime. Fish and seafood are prominent on a wide-ranging menu that includes octopus, lobster and *caldeirada* (fish soup).

Fernandes (tel: 852147). Close to the Cachalote, and a cheap alternative, this restaurant chooses to have a green canopy above the door rather than a name. The décor is clean and simple, the food modest and unembellished.

Polo Norte (tel: 852322). Opposite the Residência Calhau, this is a welcoming restaurant where you can choose between a snack bar with pine benches and a more formal dining room. A friendly ambience and the presence of locals helps compensate for a predictable menu and unexceptional view.

◆◆
RABAÇAL

One of Madeira's hidden secrets (but much loved by locals), Rabaçal is a one-house town at the eastern end of the Ribiera da Janela. If you decide to visit, take a picnic as it is quite remote.

To reach Rabaçal look for a turning north off the EN204 that crosses Paúl da Serra. This is an adventurous drive down a

Porto do Moniz

steep and tortuously winding single lane road (without crash barriers) that descends into a vivid green ravine for just over 1 mile (2km). At the end is a government-owned resthouse (not open to the public) and signposts to two *levada* walks. This is a marvellous opportunity to sample the unspoilt interior of Madeira and to appreciate the unique pleasures of *levada* walking.

The shortest walk is along the Levada do Risco to the Risco waterfall (40 minutes return) and relatively easy. You will need good footwear, though, as the paths can be very wet and slippery. Within a few minutes from the resthouse you will find the path forks. The higher route leads to the Risco waterfall. The lower route leads down to the Levada das Vinte-e-Cinco Fontes (2 hours 30 minutes return). Parts of this walk involve stretches of narrow path with nothing to hold you if you slip over the precipitous sides – not for the faint-hearted or those who suffer from vertigo.

◆
RIBEIRA DE JANELA

Janela is the Portugese word for window, and a gaping hole in the rocks of the Ilhéus da Ribeira da Janela explains the name of this tiny village a few minutes drive east of Porto do Moniz. A pull-in on its western side gives the best views.

◆
SEIXAL

Five miles (8km) west of São Vicente, Seixal is a small village famous for the steepness of its vineyards. It lies in the middle of one of the most exciting stretches of road on Madeira, running between São Vicente and Porto do Moniz. Sometimes you drive right alongside the crashing sea, sometimes you thread through damp tunnels and at other times you climb hairpin bends to skirt a sheer drop. At several points waterfalls spill down onto the road from the cliffs above – a free and natural car wash.

CENTRAL MADEIRA

A crown of mountains rises in the centre of Madeira, its peaks piercing the clouds to provide superb aerial views over the island. Climb up to the summits of Pico Ruivo or Pico do Arieiro and you will inevitably be inspired to contemplate the forces, natural or supernatural, that provoked Madeira to arise from the shimmering Atlantic some 20 million years ago. These mountain areas are remarkably accessible for both motorists and walkers, and central Madeira provides the best options for a night or two away from Funchal. Here the island's two *pousadas* (state-run inns) offer a satisfying blend of comfort and isolation, while the tranquil coastal towns of Ribeira Brava and São Vicente remain, despite new developments, the epitome of small town life. This is also where you can see Madeira at its most traditional and picturesque. In Santana the traditional thatch-roofed houses, with their brightly painted triangular facades, have been preserved in brightly painted colours.

Getting Around

There are two routes from Funchal to Madeira's north coast. The longest, but with the most impressive scenery, is to the west, via Ribeira Brava (the EN214) and Boca da Encumeada (the EN104). There is a quicker route to the east via Monte and Ribeiro Frio (the EN103). A good and full day-trip is to travel clockwise round these routes, with a diversion up to Achada do Teixeira or Pico do Arieiro.

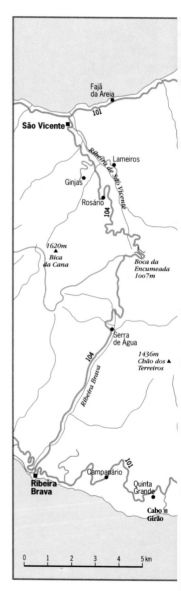

MADEIRA: CENTRAL

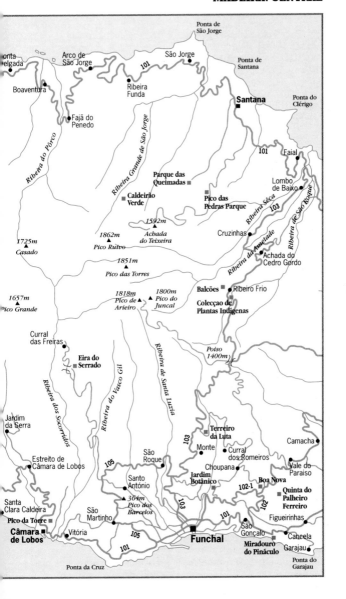

CENTRAL MADEIRA

◆◆◆
ACHADA DO TEIXEIRA ✓

Pico Ruivo, the island's highest point (6,106ft/1,862m) can be reached by a thrilling 16-mile (10-km) drive south from Santana. Look for a turn off on the eastern side of the village, next to a Shell garage. The road (the EN101-5) climbs steadily from farmland to forest, passing through the Pico das Pedras park where there are numerous picnic tables and benches. Once you get above the treeline there are glorious views back down to the coast. The road ends at Achada do Teixeira, from where a path leads up towards Pico Ruivo. If the weather is good you will be refreshed by sharp mountain air and strong sunshine. The winds can be strong up here, and the clouds come rushing in like the tide. They may spoil your fun, but more often they enhance it.

From Pico Ruivo there is a tremendous roof-of-the-world walk past peaks and crags to Pico do Arieiro, where there is a *pousada* (see **Accomodation** below) and a road back to Poiso (see **Pico do Arieiro** on page 61 for details). Close to the car park at Achada do Teixeira you will see a government resthouse (closed to the public) standing in a fenced field. If you walk behind this there are impressive views over the northeastern coast. In the foreground is a curious rock formation, not unlike a bunch of fingers but curiously called Homem-em-Pé, meaning 'Man on Foot'.

◆◆◆
BOCA DA ENCUMEADA ✓

The Encumeada Pass (3,303ft/1,007m) marks the traditional crossover point for islanders travelling between the north and south of Madeira. From here the deep valleys of Ribeira Brava and Ribeira de São Vicente cut down towards the sea in opposite directions. A road (the EN104) now covers the track that once took days to walk, creating one of the most enjoyable drives you can take on Madeira. The most dramatic approach is from Ribeira Brava, along a road that resolutely turns its back on the sea to penetrate the recesses of a forbiddingly steep-sided ravine. Sometimes a ceiling of broody clouds hides the mountains above; at other times the valley is filled with sunshine, revealing the wealth of crops that thrive in its shelter. At the sleepy village of Serra de Água the road starts to climb steeply, offering views back down to a valley floor scattered with white houses.

At Encumeada the road forks. To the west is the recently completed EN204, which runs via Lombo do Mouro to Paúl da Serra, with good views back to Madeira's central peaks. To the north the road drops gently down towards São Vicente, through a green terraced valley where visitors are welcomed with a liberal supply of picnic sites and the reassuring sight of the sea.

Besides having a bar and souvenir stalls, Encumeada is a good place to contemplate the *levada* phenomenon. Just across the road from the bar is the Levada das Rabaças. Even if you only do a short stroll along its level, flower-lined path, you will soon appreciate the appeal of *levada* walking. If you walk west (one hour return) there are memorable views down to Serra de Água, and at certain points you can see how the *levadas* wind around the hills in a single, carefully cut incision. On the opposite side of the valley the *levada* tumbles into a chute, where the water's rapid drop is exploited by a hydro-electric power station far below. (Unless you are prepared for landslides, waterfalls and small dank tunnels, it is inadvisable to try and walk the full length of Levada das Rabaças.)

Accommodation

Pousada dos Vinháticos, Serra de Água (tel: 952148). Popular with walkers and lovers of rural peace, this state-owned inn enjoys an isolated position above the village of Serra de Água. There are only 12 rooms (book well ahead) and a lounge and games room. During the day it is sporadically deluged by coach parties, but at night you can enjoy the inner peace of a starlit mountain valley. The *pousada* has an unpretentious restaurant (open to non-residents) offering Madeiran specialities like *espetada em pau de louro* (kebabs cooked on a skewer made of laurel wood), rabbit and country soups.

The stunning mountainous scenery of the interior at Pico do Arieiro

CENTRAL MADEIRA

◆◆◆ CABO GIRÃO ✓

Some 7½ miles (12km) west of Câmara de Lobos, Cabo Girão is one of the highest sea cliffs in the world, with a vertical rise of 1,902ft (580m). Near the village of Quinta Grande, a short road leads south from the EN214 to a viewing point protected by some very necessary metal railings. After summoning the courage to look at the sheer drop below, you can also enjoy panoramic views along the coast and marvel at how the islanders work fields at such perilous heights.

◆ FAIAL

Faial is a small farming village on the northeastern coast, noticeable for its tall white church with a tiered belltower. Along with São Roque do Faial and Porto da Cruz, it stands in an area of fertile, undulating countryside overshadowed by the Penha de Águia mountain. Here you can see the intensity with which Madeira's farmers use the land, with every available space given over to ambitious terracing, vegetable plots, willow groves and cattle sheds.

◆◆ PARQUE DAS QUEIMADAS

A secluded picnic and walking spot, Queimadas lies 3 miles (5km) south of Santana. Look for a turn off on its western outskirts (by a supermarket), where the road soon deteriorates into a rough track leading uphill. Passing tangles of gorse, hydrangeas and wildflowers, this winds up into the heart of a damp, enchanted forest where lichen hangs from the trees like tattered rags. Here you will find the Casa das Queimadas, a large thatched house built for government workers. Outside there are picnic tables, toilets and gurgling streams where ducks and swans cavort. Nearby is a mossy path that runs beside the Levada do Caldeirao Verde. This trails through the forest, skirting two valleys, to reach a waterfall (three to four hours return). The path can get wet and slippery and, after an hour or so, you will meet tunnels.

Shrouded by cloud, the precipitous cliffs at Cabo Girão

◆◆◆ PICO DO ARIEIRO ✓

Do not miss this chance to drive to the very top of a 5,963-ft (1,818-m) high mountain poking up in the middle of the Atlantic. Pico do Arieiro is the third highest peak on Madeira, yet one of the most accessible points on the island. From the crossroads at Poiso a road (the EN202) leads west, rising above the forests to a barren moorland grazed by sheep. Look back to the south and you will see Funchal way below, while ahead the craggy mountains rise, often threaded with ethereal wisps of cloud. At the summit there is a *pousada*, with a bar and restaurant, next to the car park (see **Accommodation** below). Near here some steps lead up to a panoramic viewpoint from where you can survey the islands – or at least a cotton-wool bed of sunlit cloud. A second viewpoint to the east of the *pousada*, the Miradouro do Juncal, looks down over the east coast.

From Pico do Arieiro you can see a path winding northwest across the mountain tops. This is an easy walk – one of the best on the island – that leads via Pico das Torres to Pico Ruivo and Achada do Teixeira. It takes about two-and-a-half hours to do (one way) – warm clothing and good footwear are essential as the winds can be cold. The walk is protected by railings but is narrow in places, with sheer drops below; it also requires passing through some narrow *levada*-like tunnels.

There are many dramatic mountain-top viewpoints and a good selection of picnic sites along the way.

Accommodation
Pousada do Pico do Arieiro
(tel: 230110). Opened in 1988, this government-owned inn offers isolated luxury on a mountain top. There are 18 comfortable rooms, a spacious lounge with large picture windows and an expensive, but good-quality, restaurant. There is a separate bar and lounge for non-residents visiting Pico do Arieiro. If you want to escape Funchal for a couple of days, the *pousada* offers a useful package that consists of a day walking from Achada do Teixiera to Pico do Arieiro, a night in the hotel with dinner, and a walk down to Santo António the next day. It costs around 13,000 escudos and includes the guide, picnics and transport.

◆ POISO

A traditional pass through the east of Madeira's mountains, Poiso stands at 4,593ft (1,400m) on the high road (the EN103) between Funchal and Faial. The surrounding land is currently being reforested.

Restaurants
Casa de Abrigo (tel: 782259). An isolated country restaurant with a friendly bar, open wood fire and cosy log-cabin atmosphere. If the weather is bad this is the ideal place to adjourn for some revitalising Madeiran soup and *espetada* (kebabs).

PONTA DELGADA

A small coastal village 5½ miles (9km) west of São Vicente, Ponta Delgada is still tuning into the modern world. With its unpainted church, cobbled roads and tiny quay, it gives a clue as to how Madeira was before all the Euro-money arrived.

RIBEIRA BRAVA

Standing at the head of the Ribeira Brava valley, this coastal town is the traditional gateway to the west of the island. Today, as tourist developments spread west from Funchal, it seems set to prosper. So far only parts of the town have been modernised, creating a delicate balance of old and new that will appeal to connoisseurs of change.

For a good preliminary view, there is a *miradouro* to the left as you approach the Ribeira Brava from Funchal. The road then winds down into the valley, where there is a seafront car park beside the Hotel Brava Mar. Here you will see an old watchtower, rather like a large chess-piece, which is decorated every Christmas with an elaborate Nativity scene.

The old streets of Ribeira Brava are to the north – take the narrow Rua do Visconde, once its main street and still full of dark, poky shops crammed with all manner of goods. Rising above the houses you will see the steeple of the São Benito church, faced with blue and white tiles. Although it was

begun in the 16th century, the church has been considerably altered and restored. At the eastern end of the town a tunnel leads through the cliffs to a fishing harbour.

Events

In October Ribeira Brava hosts a festival of Madeiran musical bands.

Accommodation

Brava Mar (tel: 952220). An unremarkable but hospitable 3-star hotel with restaurant and rooftop swimming pool, part of a modern complex that commands the town centre. There are 51 rooms, some with balcony – those at the back look out over the church and valley, with sea and car park views to the front.

Restaurants

Água Mar (tel: 951148). At the western end of town and right beside the sea. Standard Madeiran and international fare with an above average selection of desserts. Service can be slow, but the restaurant is comfortable and moderately priced.

Shopping

There is a small fruit and vegetable **market** next to the Hotel Brava Mar where it is difficult to buy anything without having to reveal your life story to its politely inquisitive stallholders. Opposite the GALP garage is the new **Lido Sol** supermarket – if you are heading north or west this is the best place to stock up with drinks, picnic ingredients and driver-soothing items. In the **Centro Comercial São Benito**

there is a souvenir shop with a good range of local items including knitted hats and socks.

◆◆
RIBEIRO FRIO

Ribeiro Frio is a forest resort on the EN103 road between Poiso and Faial. On either side of the village you will find a good choice of picnic sites set in

Ribeira Brava – the gateway to the west of the island

wooded clearings, often with tables, benches and barbecues. Some of the nicest spots are near Achada do Cedro Gordo.

Ribeiro Frio is the site of a government-run trout farm where you can walk around a series of pools containing fish in a progression of sizes. These are bordered with ornamental privet hedges beneath which, with typically Madeiran pragmatism, the workers have planted marrows and courgettes.

On the opposite side of the road is a small and conscientiously labelled Colecção de Plantas Indígenas (Collection of Indigenous Plants). Further down the hill a shop, Cold River Souvenirs, has a wide, if predictable, range of Madeira-related goods.

Just below this is the starting point for two *levada* walks along the Levada do Furado. One leads west to Balcões – you can see the *levada* running along the left-hand side of the road. It takes about 45 minutes return and culminates in an excellent view over the Ribeira da Ametade. A more difficult walk leads east along the same *levada* and the Levada da Portela. This is one of the most popular on the island because it rejoins the EN102 road near Portela. Some travel agencies offer it as an organised excursion, or you can negotiate with a taxi driver to deliver and collect you. It takes about three-and-a-half hours one way – parts of the route are unprotected and vertiginous.

Restaurants

Victor's Bar and Restaurant (tel: 575898). This occupies a wooden building overlooking the river. The bar is small with a wood fire. The restaurant is reasonably priced and offers a good range of meat dishes – and, of course, trout.

♦♦♦
SANTANA ✓

Famous for its triangular thatched houses and passionately well-kept gardens, it is easy to see why Santana has won numerous 'best-kept village' awards in the past. Next to the town hall and the O Colmo restaurant respectively stand two groups of brightly painted *palheiros* – A-shaped cottages with straw roofs that almost touch the ground. A central door leads into small living quarters, with the upper level used for storage.

These traditional houses were once more widespread around the island, but only those in Santana have been preserved. If you walk or drive around the back streets of the village you can see that many more are still in use as homes – some lovingly maintained, others declining into sheds for cows.

Events

At the end of June Santana hosts a Festa das Tosquias (Sheep-Shearing Festival), and in July a Folkore Festival with local music and dances.

Restaurants

O Colmo, Sítio do Serrado (tel: 572478). Standing beside the main road, this is the principal bar and restaurant in Santana; it also has rooms to let. At times overwhelmed by tour groups, it has a restful wooden décor and an open fire. The menu is refreshingly varied and includes lobster, snails, trout from the farm at Ribeiro Frio and goat's cheese with honey. Moderate to expensive prices.

A traditional thatched A-shaped house in Santana

◆
SÃO JORGE

São Jorge, and Arco de São Jorge to its west, are two small villages on the island's north coast. A view point at Cabanas, located halfway between the two villages, gives good views of São Jorge and the Atlantic. This stretch of coast is a popular destination for islanders driving up from Funchal at the weekend. Some arrive in racy sports cars, others in battered pick-up trucks, but all come to picnic in the surrounding woods.

Restaurant

As Cabanas, Cabanas (tel: 576291). Midway between Arco de São Jorge and São Jorge, this is a sightseer-wooing complex with a good value restaurant popular with both locals and tourists. The dining room is circular and nondescript, but the *espetada* (kebabs) are excellent. Two traditional A-shaped houses have been placed next door as a tourist attraction. The curious round houses behind As Cabanas reflect the establishment's ambition to become a motel.

Shopping

The Cabanas complex includes a spacious souvenir shop that covers the full range of Madeiran mementoes – if you have purchases of this nature to make, this is a good place to um and ah. Besides dolls, table linen, pottery, knitted garments and countless items inscribed with 'Madeira', there is an exhaustive range of local drinks. If you are looking indecisive, the manageress will help by graphically describing what *poncha* (the local rum) does to men, and what *maracujá* (passion fruit liqueur) does to her. After that it is impossible to resist buying one or the other and testing its effects for yourself.

◆◆
SÃO VICENTE

Situated at the head of the São Vicente valley, this northern coastal town is split into two parts. The older houses lie a short distance inland, sheltering from the sea winds, while modern developments, principally hotels and restaurants, line the shore. The sea here can sometimes be very rough, with Atlantic rollers crashing onto the pebbled beach. When enough driftwood and sugar cane has washed up, rows of bonfires are lit to clear the rubbish – an eery and compelling sight if you happen to be around at the time.
The old town, protected by mountains that loom over it like guardians, has a quiet charm. A simple parish church provides the focus for a gaggle of pedestrianised streets full of small, sell-everything shops. Opposite its entrance is the Bar-Pastelaria Estoril – a good place to pause for a coffee and cake while musing upon the unhurried lifestyle of the villagers.
If you are driving down from Boca da Encumeada you will notice another church set high on a hill, Nossa Senhora de Fátima. This was built in the 1940s and is actually a chapel with an unusually high clocktower. Down by the mouth of the river, next to a concrete bridge, there is another eye-catching chapel constructed at the end of the 17th century. At Christmas the cross on top of its rocks is poignantly lit up in red lights with white rigging.

Accommodation
Estalagem do Mar (tel: 842615). A self-contained 4-star hotel used by both businessmen and tour groups. Right beside the sea with dramatic cliffs rising behind, it has 41 rooms, two restaurants, a swimming pool, sun terrace, sauna, and squash and tennis courts.
Estalagem Praia Mar (tel: 842383). Opened in 1992, this is a 20-room hotel close to the seashore with a bright, homely character. There is a large restaurant and some bedrooms have balconies.

Restaurants
Quebra Mar (tel: 842338). This is a circular cream building that looks like an oil refinery. Nevertheless, it is the most promising place to eat in São Vicente, but with a slightly less unimaginative menu than its competitors, the **Estalagems Calamar**, **do Mar** and **Praia Mar**. If none of these appeal, two small seafront bars, the **Caravela** and the **Virgilio**, provide cheap and cheerful alternatives.

The red roofs of São Vicente's old town nestle beneath the terraced green slopes of the protecting mountains

THE EAST

The east of Madeira is characterised by a series of long river valleys sloping southeastwards to the sea. In the north a hilly neck of land

MADEIRA: EAST

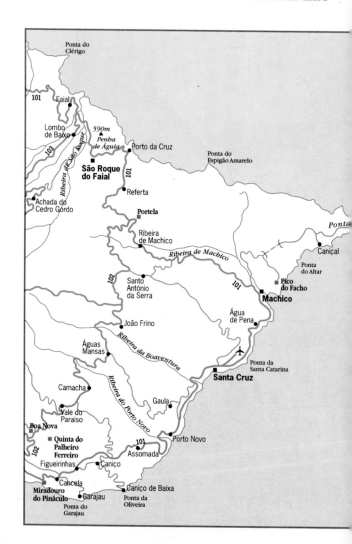

extends into the sea, the Ponta de São Lourenço.

This is the most farmed and developed part of the island, where the changing lifestyle of

the Madeirans is most apparent. At the start of this century Machico, the island's second largest settlement, had four working sugar-cane mills – now all closed. Until 1981 Caniçal was a busy whaling station whose fishermen had slaughtered over 5,000 whales in the previous 40 years. The island's wicker industry, centred in Camacha since the mid-19th century, is now threatened by competition from the Far East. Nevertheless this area is striving to become a flagship of the new Madeira, and is already home to a modern airport, a tax-free industrial zone at Caniçal, several holiday developments and two golf courses.

Getting Around

Eastern Madeira is the easiest part of the island to tour. The landscape is not so mountainous, and a good fast road (the EN101) connects Funchal to the airport and Machico. A popular round trip from Funchal is to take the high road (the EN102) to Camacha and Santo António da Serra then return along the coast. A detour out to Ponta de São Lourenço is easily included.

◆◆◆

CAMACHA

Camacha is a prosperous highland village 6½ miles (10km) northeast of Funchal, and the centre of Madeira's wickerwork industry. Travelling round the surrounding valleys you will see the groves of well-pruned willow trees that provide the raw material for what has become a sizeable export product. The long green

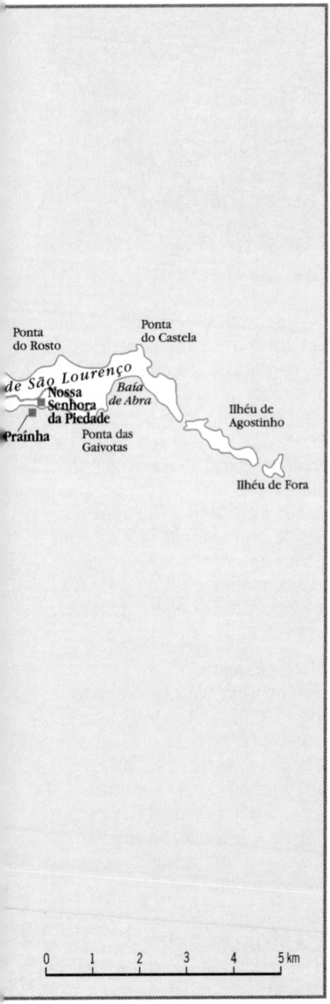

Ponta do Rosto

Ponta do Castela

de São Lourenço

Nossa Senhora da Piedade

Baía de Abra

Ilhéu de Agostinho

Prainha

Ponta das Gaivotas

Ilhéu de Fora

0 1 2 3 4 5 km

canes are cut in spring then soaked, peeled and graded according to their strength and size. These are then made into baskets, furniture and domestic goods, mainly by families working at home in sheds, workshops or the open air. The development of this craft, which now employs some 2,000 islanders, owes a lot to the taste for cane furniture that the British acquired from their Far Eastern colonies. Their presence in Madeira created a demand for wicker furniture in houses and hotels, which supplanted a tradition of making baskets for use by farmers and labourers.

Weaving wickerwork

Events

Camacha boasts one of the best-known folk-dancing groups in the islands and frequently stages cultural events. In October there is a Festa da Macã (Apple Festival).

Shopping

If you want to buy wickerwork, make straight for Camacha's central square and the **O Relógio** emporium. The building is divided into four floors, with the top one given over to a restaurant that has superb views of the Ilhas Desertas. On the ground floor there is what amounts to a wickerwork supermarket, with goods piled so high it is a job to get round. Bottle-holders, plant-holders, bread baskets, picnic baskets, handbags, trays – the prices are very reasonable and it is hard to leave without something taking your fancy. Stairs then lead down to two lower levels. The first is full of furniture – armchairs,

bedheads, linen baskets – plus an impressive menagerie of large wicker animals, including reindeer, a giraffe, an elephant and several birds. Unfortunately these are not for sale, but instead stand as testimony to the skill of local weavers. On the lowest floor you can watch these craftsmen at work – some stripping and preparing the cane, others winding it round chairs and stools with amazing speed.

Restaurants

A Cornélia, Vale do Paraiso (tel: 792892). A mile (1.6km) south of Camacha, this is a simple roadside restaurant serving no-nonsense home cooking at reasonable prices. Meals are served in the sun-lounge or the small dining room with pine tables.

◆

CANIÇAL

The easternmost village on Madeira, Caniçal can be

reached by driving through a tunnel to the east of Machico on the EN101-3. Until 1981 this was the principal whaling station on the island and the atmosphere here, and along Ponta de São Lourenço, is noticeably different from the rest of Madeira. Before the completion of the tunnel in 1956, the village could only be reached by boat or by a series of narrow cliffside paths. This isolation is said to explain the predominance of Jewish and Moorish features in the local population, a legacy of the slaves and settlers who lived here in previous centuries. With the end of whaling, Caniçal has developed new interests. It remains a fishing port but, ironically, is now earmarked as a base for marine conservation. A Free Port has been established on its outskirts, offering tax advantages to foreign businesses but doing little for the landscape. If you drop down through the village towards the sea you will find a small shed next to the boatyard selling souvenirs carved from whalebone. Nearby is the Museu da Baleia, a museum devoted to the days of whaling. Besides displaying harpoons, scrimshaws (whalebone carvings) and whalebone furniture, there are photographic portraits of the men who undertook this pursuit and a 45-minute video (in English, German or French) of a whale hunt that took place off Caniçal in 1978.
Open: Tuesday–Sunday 10.00–18.00hrs.

Events

On the third Sunday in September a festival is held in honour of the port's patroness, Nossa Senhora da Piedade. A statue of Our Lady is carried down to the shore from the chapel on Ponta de São Lourenço, then taken to Caniçal in a procession of decorated fishing boats.

The fishing port of Caniçal

◆
CANIÇO

Six miles (10km) east of Funchal, Caniço is a sprawling town with an imposing 18th-century church at its centre. From here a road (take the Rua Dr F Peres) winds south to Caniço de Baixa, a rapidly developing seaside resort popular with German visitors. If you like to go diving, this is the place to come.

Accommodation
Roca Mar, Caniço de Baixa (tel: 934334). A new, quality 4-star hotel perched on the cliffs with gardens, restaurant and swimming pool. All 37 rooms have balconies with sea views. Sports facilities include a diving club, volley-ball court and mini-golf course.

◆◆
GARAJAU

On the coast between Funchal and Caniço, Garajau gets its name from the large number of terns (*garajaus*) that nest here. Today it is a modern residential and tourist village. If you continue towards the sea the road culminates in a headland, the Ponta da Garajau, where there is a large statue of Christ with arms outstretched. Erected in 1927, it is similar to more famous statues in Lisbon and Rio de Janeiro.
Beside this headland an unsignposted cobbled road leads off to the west, descending steeply down the cliffs to the sea. This is a good place to visit at sunset, when the evening sun burnishes the rocks whose sloping strata resemble a slice of chocolate

Statue of Christ at Garajau

cake. At the bottom there is a pebbled beach with a jumble of fishermen's houses, beach huts and summerhouses built beside the cliffs. Constructed with great individuality, they make a striking contrast to the towering skyscrapers of Funchal further round the coast.

Accommodation
Dom Pedro Garajau (tel: 934421). This is a 4-star resort hotel with 282 rooms, mostly apartments with kitchen facilities. There are three swimming pools, a restaurant, gardens, disco, shops and an entertainment programme.

◆◆
MACHICO

Machico is where Zarco and Teixeira, the official discoverers of Madeira, first landed in 1420, though according to local legend the town was actually founded almost a century earlier by an Englishman called Robert Machim. He and his lover, Anne d'Arfet, had eloped from Bristol aboard a ship bound for Portugal, but they were caught in a storm and shipwrecked off Madeira. The survivors reached the bay at Machico, but Anne soon died. Heartbroken, Robert erected a large cedarwood cross above her grave. A few days later he died too and was buried by her side. The rest of the crew eventually escaped by raft, but were caught by Moorish pirates and condemned to slavery. A Spanish slave then overheard their story and, on his release, spread news of Madeira's discovery. It was rumours like these that inspired Zarco to set off on his voyage of exploration. When he landed on the island he did indeed find a cedarwood cross, inspiring him to give Madeira's first settlement the name of Machico, a corruption of Robert Machim's name. Today Machico is the most important town in Madeira after Funchal, with some 13,000 inhabitants. Once a major sugar-cane centre (a chimney from one of its mills still stands beside the river), it is now occupied with fishing, agriculture and light industry. Despite the arrival of the domineering Dom Pedro Baía hotel, it has not sold out to tourism. Much of the seafront, which would be considered prime real estate elsewhere, is given over to a football pitch, and you can still find plots of bananas and guavas dotted around the town centre, lending the place an air of greenery.

Sightseeing

Machico is an interesting town but, with the exception of August and September, quieter than many visitors expect. The Ribeira de Machico divides it in two, flowing down to a wide pebbled beach with some black sand. Unfortunately many of the town's churches and historical buildings are often closed or in private ownership, and while there are plans to develop the potential of these sights, for the moment the best way to enjoy Machico is to just wander and wonder.

South of the River

A cemetery may seem an unlikely place to start a walk, but if you are staying at the Dom Pedro Baía you should certainly take a look at what is, poignantly, one of the most colourful places in Machico. Just downhill from the hotel, on the left, the cemetery dates from 1885 and its painted metal crosses, ornately-framed photos and overwhelming displays of the island's spectacular flowers are a homage to life in this corner of the Madeira. From here you can turn right down an avenue lined with tall trees, the Praça do Dr José António d'Almada. On the right is the west wall of the triangular Forte do Amparo, built in 1706 after repeated attacks on the port by pirates. Today it is used by customs officials but is scheduled to become a museum. Turning left at the bottom, past the Mercado Velho restaurant, you reach a narrow shopping street that leads to Machico's central square.

THE EAST

Here taxi-drivers, shoeshines and old men chat in the shade of ancient plane trees. In the centre of the square is a statue of Machico's first governor, Tristão Vaz Teixeira. Behind is the Igreja Matriz de Machico, a parish church dating from the 15th century. The marble columns on its side portal were donated by King Manuel I, and there are evocative 17th-century tombstones on the floor by the main entrance. On the far side of the square is an elaborate drinking fountain shaped like a shell, one of several around the town that reflect the civic zeal of the late 1920s. From here a bridge leads across the river, its grassy bed often grazed by cows.

North of the River

Known as Banda d'Além, this area of low houses and narrow cobbled streets is where Machico's fishermen and their families once lived. Walking seaward you pass a small chapel on the left that has stood here since the days of the first colonists, though damage by fire and flood has necessitated its rebuilding several times. In 1803 floods inundated the church, sweeping a crucifix out to sea. This was later rescued when it was found floating in the waters off Madeira by an American ship. After this the chapel was dedicated to Nosso Senhor dos Milagres (Our Lord of Miracles).

Bearing left you pass Machico's boatyards, from where you can follow the Rua do Leiria around the bay. This lane is often used by fishermen to mend the long lines they use to catch *espada*, which can lie at a depth of up to 2,500ft (762m). Once you have seen the lines strung from tree to tree, with individual hooks spaced at regular intervals down their length, you will appreciate the work required to get this elusive fish onto your dinner plate. At the end of the road is a small jetty with good views back across Machico bay. Nearby some steps lead up to what was once the Forte de São João Baptista. Constructed in 1708, it was turned into a hospital during a cholera epidemic in 1910 and is now a private residence.

Events

On the last Sunday in August Machico celebrates the Festa do Santíssimo Sacramento (Festival of the Holy Sacrament) with the lighting of a huge bonfire. On 8 and 9 October a festival is held in honour of Nosso Senhor dos Milagres with a torchlit procession from the chapel.

Accommodation

Atlantis, Água de Pena (tel: 965811). A luxurious 5-star high-rise hotel to the south of Machico. Facilities include a heated indoor pool, an *à la carte* restaurant, nightclub, cinema, tennis courts and health club. The hotel is part of the Matur holiday complex, a self-contained resort with shops, restaurants, gardens and swimming pools. The accommodation is in apartments or villas.

Dom Pedro Baía (tel: 965751). This 4-star high-rise hotel has

218 rooms, many with good views over the bay. Despite external signs of wear and tear, the hotel is comfortable and welcoming, with a full entertainment programme. There is a restaurant, swimming pool and sun terrace.

Residêncial Machico, Praça do Salazar (tel: 966511). A small pension in a new development beside the bandstand.

Restaurants
Mercado Velho, Rua do Mercado (tel: 962370). A pleasant restaurant in Machico's old market with an enclosed terrace ideal for a drink, snack or a meal *al fresco*. Mature trees and the market's old marble fountain make this a cool refuge from the summer heat.

Marina, Rua do Leiria (tel: 966625). A new restaurant, specialising in fish, close to the boatyard. Moderate to expensive prices.

O Facho, Praça do Salazar (tel: 962786). One of the livelier places in a quiet town. You can have a snack at the bar or dine in the formal restaurant next door.

Pastelaria Galã, Rua da Mercado (tel: 965720). Worth visiting both for its excellent cakes and its small and extremely popular restaurant.

Shopping
Wine Shop, Rua General António Teixiera d'Aguiar 12 (tel: 962599). A small helpful shop with a good selection of Madeira wine and local spirits. Be sure to look in the window of No 13 opposite, which has an intriguing display of suitably dusty vintage bottles – some

over 150 years old.

Souvenir Machim, Edificio Paz, Rua do Ribeirinho (tel: 963324). A wide choice of Madeiran souvenirs including embroidered blouses, wickerwork, fans, bags and table linen. The tourist office is in the same block.

◆
PICO DO FACHO
To the north of Machico, and just before the tunnel that leads to Ponta de São Lourenço, a road winds out to the summit of Pico do Facho. This mountain get its name from the beacons (*fachos*) lit to warn the islanders of approaching pirates. From here there are panoramic views across the Machico valley, up to the island's central peaks and out along Ponta de São Lourenço. All these, however, are upstaged by the mesmerising sight of aeroplanes taking off and landing on the remarkably short runway at Santa Catarina airport.

◆◆
PONTA DE SÃO LOURENÇO
Ponta de São Lourenço is the easternmost point on Madeira, a narrow peninsula of dry, sandy land that provides a foretaste of the landscape on Porto Santo (in fact it is linked underwater to the even more barren Ilhas Desertas). The peninsula can only be reached via a tunnel to the north of Machico, along a road (the EN101-3) that leads past Caniçal to Ponta das Gaivotas. Along its southern shore is Praínha, the only sandy beach on Madeira. The sand is black

and the small beach can only be reached by a steep walk down from the nearby chapel of Nossa Senhora de Piedade. To the north a road leads up to Ponta do Rosto, where there are colourful views out across blood-red cliffs and deep-blue waters.

The road ends above the Baía de Abra, where the car park is usually enlivened by an old man selling souvenirs carved from whalebone. These are left over from the days when Caniçal was a busy whaling station. From here there are good, breezy walks out across the headlands.

♦♦
SANTA CRUZ

Before the building of the airport, Santa Cruz was a peaceful town of yellow and white houses tucked away on Madeira's east coast. Despite the cars zooming along the new road above and the jets roaring overhead, it still has an air of dignity. Three historic buildings in particular contribute to its sense of bygone charm.

Standing in a central square is the whitewashed parish church of São Salvador, one of the oldest on the island, dating from 1533. It is shaded by *til* trees (*Ocotea foetens*), last remnants of the island's former forest cover.

Across the square is the restored 16th-century Câmara Municipal (Town Hall), which still has some gracious windows in the ornate Manueline style. A short walk to the east is a magisterial grey and white courthouse framed by contemplative gardens.

Down by the seafront there is a covered market and, nearby, a pebble beach with a seawater pool, the Praia das Palmeiras.

♦♦
SANTO ANTÓNIO DA SERRA

This small plateaux stands over 2,200ft (671m) above sea level and its refreshing climate has made it a favourite summer retreat for Funchal's wealthier residents. Usually known simply as Santo da Serra, it can be reached by turning off the

EN102-3 road 3 miles (5km) south of Portela, taking the EN207. Along this road you can see the gates and nameplates of the grand *quintas* (estates) and villas that have been built around Santo da Serra.
Just below the village square is the Parque do Santo da Serra, its entrance marked by wooden gates. Once owned by the Blandy family, this is now open to the public and gives a good idea of the stately properties in the area. Its well-kept gardens lead down to a viewpoint

The magisterial grey and white courthouse in Santa Cruz

overlooking the Machico valley. There is also a children's playground, mini-golf course, tennis court and a small zoo displaying several birds of prey, deer and even a kangaroo.
To the south of the village is the 27-hole Santo da Serra golf course which hosts the Madeira Open. If you continue descending towards Água de Pena, you can enjoy good views of the three Ilhas Desertas.

PORTO SANTO

Porto Santo was the first of the Madeiran islands to be discovered, and it is not hard to imagine the day in 1418 when Zarco and Teixeira landed on its magnificent beach. Soon neglected in favour of the larger and more cultivable island of Madeira, and always vulnerable to attack by pirates, it has remained in a state of weary innocence, like a friend whose career never quite took off.

Even today, Porto Santo is a blissfully undemanding place to visit. It has only one attraction: a 4½-mile (7-km) long pale sandy beach that stretches the length of the south coast. Serenely deserted in winter, this fills with activity in summer – a Funchal–on–Sea where the Madeirans come to enjoy some seaside fun.

Walking along this sandy shore, there is a good chance that you will be following in the footsteps of Christopher Columbus. While the exact facts of the explorer's life will be forever clouded with controversy, it is known that he married Filipa Moniz, the daughter of Porto Santo's first governor, Bartolomeu Perestrello. Columbus is thought to have visited the islands as early as 1478, having been commissioned by traders in Lisbon to purchase sugar. Romantics say that seeds and wood washed up on the shore of Porto Santo, indicating the possible existence of land the other side of the Atlantic, inspired him to sail west.

The celebrations for the 500th anniversary of Columbus's discovery of America in 1492 spurred the Portuguese into recognising Porto Santo's contribution to world history. In Vila Baleira, the island's main town, you can now visit the house where the great man is said to have lived.

Porto Santo's other attractions result from the island's contrast with Madeira. The countryside is low-lying and arid – a landscape of windmills, donkeys and motorbikes, where reforestation has greened the hills and the cattle need not be cooped up in sheds for fear that they will fall down the steep hillsides. As one local brochure puts it, this is the 'Island of Rest'.

Getting Around

While many visitors are content to just lie on Porto Santo's excellent beach, it is worth making a tour of the rest of the island. The simplest way is by taxi. A tour normally takes around two hours and will cover the main sights, excluding Pico de Ana Ferreira where the road is poor. The trip will cost about 4,000 escudos, but agree a price first. Many of the island's drivers speak good English and can be informative guides.

Hiring a car for a day is another option though it does cost significantly more. This will give you the freedom to linger in remote parts of the island, and to tackle some of its rougher roads. Be sure to have a picnic on board, or at least some water – hire cars on Porto Santo get a good thrashing, and the chances of their breaking down are higher than usual. About 1,000 escudos worth of petrol should be enough to complete a lap of the island. This can be done in two tours: one east of Vila Baleira, the island's main town, driving in an anti-clockwise circle around the island's highest hill, Pico do Facho; the other west to Ponta da Calheta. A third option is to join a tour organised by a local travel agency, such as Blandy Brothers, Avenida Dr Manuel Pestana Júnior, Vila Baleira (tel: 982676). These require a minimum of four people and cost about 1800 escudos.

VILA BALEIRA
Sometimes called Porto Santo, Vila Baleira is the only large town on the island. The ferry to and from Funchal moors up at the Porto de Abrigo, 1 mile (1.6km) to the east of the town. The airport is a 10-minute taxi drive to the west. For a map and information on the island, visit the tourist office in the Edifício da Delegação Governo Regional (near the main square).

Sightseeing
Don't get too excited. Vila Baleira is not a place to clock up

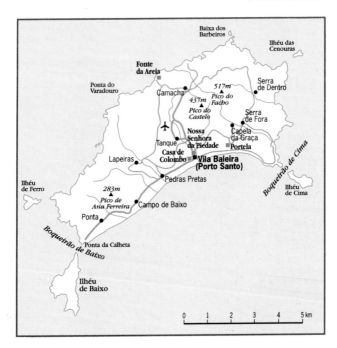

great monuments, just a small town where the best thing to do is sit in a sunny bar and savour the atmosphere of life on a semi-desert island. The Café Baiana in Rua Dr Nuno S Teixeira is a favourite with both locals and visitors, and it occupies a commanding position next to the town's central square, the Largo do Pelourinho. Surrounded by palm trees, the square contains a mosaic of black and white pebbles in the shape of a compass. You hardly need help to get your bearings – just walk towards the seafront and you'll find Vila Baleira's two 'sights' in the Rua Infante D Henrique – a bust of Christopher Columbus and a very modern 'Monument to the Discoverers' (visiting it will help you understand why the locals call it the 'Cake of Soap').

CASA DE COLOMBO

Rua Cristovão Colombo 12, Vila Baleira

This small museum is devoted to Christopher Columbus. A miscellany of pottery, tools, furniture and models is used to recreate the house where the explorer is thought to have lived. Early maps of the Americas and Madeira are displayed, along with historical prints depicting exceedingly romantic views of the arrival of Europeans in the Indies. There is also an amusing collection of wildly differing portraits of the great man ranging in date from the 16th to the 20th centuries – some saw him as a long-chinned grandee, others as a grey-bearded sage.
Open: Monday–Friday 10.00–12.00 and 14.00–17.30hrs.

FONTE DA AREIA

This 'Fountain in the Sands' is reached via the village of Camacha, from where a road leads west towards the sea. Today it is a sacred tap, set in stone with great civic pride in 1843. On an island with few permanent water supplies, the continuing importance of this natural spring is evident from the people who still arrive by car to fill up plastic containers. Nearby, the sandstone cliffs have been eroded into shapes resembling moth-eaten calico.

NOSSA SENHORA DA PIEDADE

Largo do Pelourinho, Vila Baleira

Porto Santo's principal church, recently restored, has blue and white *azulejos* tiles on the main façade and dates from the 17th century – a replacement for an earlier church destroyed by pirates in 1667.

PICO DO CASTELO

Pico do Castelo rises to the west of the island's highest peak, Pico do Facho (1,696ft/517m). Both these volcanic cones provide excellent views over Porto Santo. There are two roads that approach these peaks: one from Vila Baleira via Dragoal and another further north that passes the island's military barracks. Either way, you will reach a cobbled road that winds up to Terra Larga where there is a picnic area with benches, tables and a barbecue. Surveying the island, the eye is inevitably caught by

Porto Santo's chief attraction – its long and sandy beach

the airport, where large white letters have been laid out beside the runway to reassure pilots that, yes, this scrap of land really is PORTO SANTO. The road continues round to Pico do Castelo, from where there are views to the north of the island. Both here and at Terra Larga there are easy walks through fragrant pines, or you can hike to the summit of Pico do Facho. In previous centuries beacons were lit here to warn that hostile ships had been sighted, and you may come across the odd rusty cannon left from its castle.

◆◆
PICO DE ANA FERREIRA
If coming from Vila Baleira, turn right shortly after passing the Hotel Porto Santo at Campo de Baixo. The road is signposted to Pedreira, the Portuguese word for quarry – a description better applied to the condition of this

track than to the volcanic rock formation you are seeking. Turn left when the road forks by some farm buildings and you will reach a curious wall of rock patterned like organ pipes. On the way back you will see a white chapel with palm trees, the Capela do São Pedro which dates from the 18th century.

◆◆
PONTA DA CALHETA
There is probably no better way to enjoy Porto Santo than to take a taxi out to Ponta da Calheta then walk back along the beach. The island's southwestern tip attracts both sunbathers and fishermen, and in summer there is a bar and restaurant here, the Pôr do Sol (tel: 984380).
If you are driving, or fancy a good walk, look for a rough

track to the right shortly before reaching the Ponta da Calheta (signposted to the Hipocampo). This leads up to Pico das Flores, from where there is a good view back across the island and out to the Ilhéu de Baixo. If the weather is fine you can see across to the Ilhas Desertas and Madeira.

PORTELA

One mile (1.6km) east of Vila Baleira, this viewpoint is heralded by an avenue of palm trees and a windmill. From here you can look west down the length of Porto Santo's beach and east to the pointed Pico de Baixo and the Ilhéu de Cima, on which there is a lighthouse. On the way here you will see a white chapel set against the hills, Nossa Senhora da Graça, built in 1951.

SERRA DE DENTRO

Serra de Fora and the long valley of Serra de Dentro lie on the eastern slopes of Pico do Facho. Here farmhouses, stone walls and abandoned terraces testify to the islanders' long struggle to make a living from the land. Sheep and cattle are still grazed on these hills, but the problems of soil erosion are self-evident. Although new reservoirs and afforestation schemes have been established as counter-measures, the landscape remains deserted – hence it is a quiet place to walk and picnic.

Accommodation

Porto Santo, Campo de Baixo (tel: 982381). A low-rise, self-contained 4-star hotel to the west of Vila Baleira. Close to the beach, it has lawns, sunbathing terraces, a swimming pool, restaurant and sports facilities, including tennis courts and windsurfing. This has long been considered the island's premier hotel, and many guests never leave its grounds.

Luamar, Cabeço da Ponta (tel: 984103). Opened in 1992, this is a well-designed 4-star apartment hotel 2½ miles (4km) west of Vila Baleira. Built on three floors, each suite has a kitchenette, sitting room, bedroom and balcony. Right next to the beach, with a large pool and spacious terraces, it is ideal for families who like to cater for themselves. There are also facilities for visitors with disabilities.

For budget accommodation, there are several pensions on the island, including the **Palmeiras**, Avenida Henrique Vieira de Castro, Vila Baleira (tel: 982112) and the **Asia Mar**, Campo de Baixo (tel: 983683) which also has a pleasant Chinese/Indonesian restaurant. There is also a municipal campsite (Parque de Campismo) on the western edge of Vila Baleira (tel: 984160).

Restaurants

O Forno, Rampa da Fontinha, Vila Baleira (tel: 985141). Reasonably priced, friendly restaurant serving grilled meats including *espetada* (kebab) and *picado* (small, spicy chunks of beef), plus *bolo de caco* (bread cooked on a hot stone oven) served with garlic butter.

Mar e Sol, Campo de Baixo (tel: 982269). A fish restaurant close to the beach, popular with holidaymakers from the nearby Hotel Porto Santo.

Toca do Pescador, Salões (tel: 984442). Specialising in fish and seafood, this shanty-like shack lies a short drive to the northwest of Vila Baleira.

Teodorico, Serra de Fora (tel: 982257). Small *espetada* (kebab) restaurant to the east of Vila Baleira. Ring to check that it is open before setting out.

Bar Torres, Camacha (tel: 984373). A small, homely affair with a vine-covered terrace, on the right as you drive down towards Fonte da Areia. Both this and the nearby **Estrela do Norte** (tel: 984365) specialise in chicken. Advance booking is essential.

Shopping

Porto Santo has few shops of interest and most islanders make regular trips by ferry to shop in Funchal. Near the jetty there is a souvenir stall housed in an old windmill. Fortunately the island does maintain the Madeiran talent for making cakes. The best selection is in the **Pastelaria e Boutique de Pão Sousa & Fillio**, 57 Rua João Gonçalves Zarco. If you need a supermarket, there is a good one in the Avenida Dr Manuel Pestana Júnior called **Nova Esperanca**.

Porto Santo windmill

*Statuesque date palms provide
shade in Vila Baleira*

Sport

Sports and activities on the
island are available during the
summer months through the
Porto Santo hotel (see above).
For fishing trips and sightseeing
excursions by boat contact a
local travel agency, such as
Blandy Brothers (tel: 982676)
or **Star** (tel: 982459) both in
Avenida Dr Manuel Pestana
Júnior, Vila Baleira.
For diving and boat trips
contact **Urs Moser Diving
Centre**, 5 Rua João Gonçalves
Zarco, Vila Baleira (tel: 982162).
Bicycles and motorbikes can be
hired from the same company,
near the new GALP garage.

Horseriding and tuition is
available at the **Quinta dos
Profetas**, Sítio da Ponta (tel:
983165) in the southwestern
corner of the island.

Nightlife

Porto Santo's appeal as a
summer holiday resort explains
why a quiet town like Vila
Baleira can support four discos.
The most central are **Big Boy**
on Rua João Santana and
Challenger in Rua D Estêvão
de Alencastre. **Ventanias** lies
east of the town in the Vale do
Touro, while **Porão**, which can
hold 1,000 people, is by the
beach. There is one cinema in
Vila Baleira, the **Cine-Porto
Santo** in Rua Dr Nuno S
Teixeira.

Peace and Quiet

Wildlife and Countryside in the Madeiran Archipelago by Paul Sterry

Introduction

The combination of stunning scenery and an equable climate have made Madeira a popular holiday destination for over a century. A good road network ensures that, nowadays, much of the island can be reached with ease and hiking is also popular among those seeking a flavour of wild Madeira. Although man's effect on the native flora and fauna has been nothing short of devastating, a natural history trip is nonetheless rewarding. A good range of wildlife can be seen even during a short visit and the island's floral element has been boosted by the introduction of vast numbers of plants from around the world. These provide colourful displays around the year.

Madeira is famous for its dramatic and, in parts, inaccessible rocky terrain which is volcanic in origin. Looking at a map of the island, a ridge runs along its backbone from Ponta de São Lourenço in the east to the northwest point at Ponta do Tristão. It rises to over 6,000ft (1,800m) to the north of Funchal and forms a wide, central plateau in the west of the island. Running towards the sea in both northerly and southerly directions are a series of ridges, separated by steep ravines and gorges known as *ribeiras*.

Streams cascade down these ravines, some of them ending as boulder beaches on the coast – there is only one natural, sandy beach. Most of the ridges end as sheer cliffs, some of which are among the highest in the world. Indeed, sea cliffs surround most of the coast giving the island the look of an impregnable fortress when viewed from the sea.

The Madeiran archipelago is situated less than 400 miles (640km) from the coast of North Africa. However, the islands' oceanic position and the trade winds, invariably from the northeast, have a profoundly moderating influence on the climate: summers are never too hot and winters are mild. These climatic factors, together with the island's topography, ensure a fairly predictable weather pattern. Typically, a day will start with clear skies. Clouds, created by condensation from

PEACE AND QUIET

the rising, warmed air, form before midday and blanket the mountains – it pays to set off early when exploring the interior of Madeira.

Generally speaking, the climate is better, at least from a tourist's point of view, on the south side: cloudy conditions are more prevalent and rainfall is higher on the northern slope. However, this has its compensations as the wildlife interest in the north of the island is, in many ways, greater. Since the discovery of Madeira in 1418, man has had a profoundly adverse effect on the native elements of the flora and fauna. Once cloaked in dense forest – Ilha da Madeira means Island of Wood – settlers immediately set about clearing these by starting fires that certainly smouldered for months, perhaps years. The native laurel forests have now dwindled to small pockets which are fully protected by law and which still harbour interesting plants and animals. Agricultural land dominates most of the lowlands with vines, bananas, avocados, potatoes and sugar cane being among the many crops.

Porto Santo is the only other inhabited island in the Madeiran archipelago, lying to the northeast of the main island. The terrain is less imposing than Madeira itself, the island being lower and flatter and, consequently, the climate is much drier and warmer. The presence of a sandy beach makes it popular with sun-lovers. The uninhabited islands known as the Ilhas Desertas lie due south of the eastern tip of Madeira. Home to breeding seabirds, they are, to all intents and purposes, inaccessible. However, the birds they support can be seen feeding in the waters surrounding the main islands. The last group of islands in the archipelago, the Wild Islands (Selvagens), are even more distant and inaccessible.

Leste Winds

For most of the Madeiran year, the climate is moderated by the sea and the northeasterly trade winds. Occasionally, however, during the summer months, the winds change direction and come straight from the Sahara – these are the *leste* winds. During these albeit brief *leste* periods, which may only last a day or so, the temperature soars and the humidity plummets. Migrant birds sometimes accompany the winds and swarms of locusts have even arrived.

Boca da Encumeada

Spectacular mountains and woodland in the centre of the island.

The Boca da Encumeada can be reached by road by driving south from São Vicente or north from Ribeira Brava. It lies roughly midway between the two and the north summit is at 3,303ft (1,007m); on clear days the views are spectacular. Heading south from the highest point, stop off at various points along the wooded valley. Look for birds such as chaffinches, firecrests, robins, blackbirds and perhaps a buzzard soaring overhead.

Colourful butterflies abound, like the well-named painted lady

Cabo Girão
Cliffs to the west of Funchal on the south coast.
A winding road heads from Funchal to Cabo Girão where spectacular cliffs and views can be found. Birdwatchers should look for plain and pallid swifts, kestrels, rock pigeons and rock sparrows.

Funchal
Madeira's capital.
The gardens of Funchal are one of the great glories of Madeira. Almost every house has a garden of one sort or another providing colour and foliage throughout the year. Remnants of the once-widespread native flora, such as the dragon tree or the large viper's bugloss, *Echium nervosum*, can be found as well as introduced species such as bignonias, flame trees,

coral trees, bougainvilleas, tamarisks, poinsettias and oleanders. Colourful butterflies, such as painted lady, red admiral, clouded yellow and monarch – the latter a colonist from America – can be seen visiting the flowers alongside the day-flying hummingbird hawk moth. Birdwatchers should look for songbirds such as canaries, blackbirds, robins and blackcaps.
Particular areas worth visiting in Funchal for wildlife include the Jardim de Santa Catarina, where trees and a lake offer peace and quiet, and the Jardim de São Francisco (the Municipal Gardens) where the trees and shrubs include dragon trees and native laurels. Away from the centre of town, the world famous Jardim Botânico (Botanical Gardens) boast hundreds of plants from around the world, planted on landscaped terraces.

Paúl da Serra
A high level plateau in the west of the island.

Paúl da Serra lies at around 4,921ft (1,500m) above sea level and is, not surprisingly, sometimes shrouded in mist and low cloud. On sunny days, however, the moorland vegetation – comprising species such as tree heathers, brooms, gorses, bilberry and strawberry tree – can be

The shy goldfinch

explored. Lizards scurry at ground level and birdwatchers should look for species such as linnets and goldfinches. You might even be lucky enough to see a Berthelot's pipit, a rather sombre, grey-brown bird that prefers to run along the ground. The Madeiran islands, along with the Canaries and the Salvagens, are its only home.

Pico do Arieiro

Spectacular mountains to the north of Funchal.

To reach Pico do Arieiro, drive north from Funchal on the road to Ribeiro Frio and fork off left at Poiso. The views are spectacular and there are walks in several directions, including one northwards to Pico Ruivo, the highest point on the island. Moorland vegetation, comprising mainly bilberry, covers much of the area and here is another chance to look for Berthelot's pipit. Pico Ruivo can also be approached by driving south from Santana to Achada do Teixeira.

Pockets of the island's original laurel forest can be found along this route and in a few other places along the northern side of the island. The habitat is home to one of the most endangered birds on Madeira, the long-toed pigeon. For much of the year, its diet comprises the berries of laurel and other native trees and so woodlands comprising introduced species, such as pines, are of little value to it. Long-toed pigeons are only found on Madeira and the Canary Islands.

Ponta de São Lourenço

The easternmost point of the island.

A road leads along the peninsula. From the end, walk around the coast to view the lighthouse. Seabirds, such as Cory's and Manx shearwaters, can sometimes be seen offshore. During the winter months, October to March, herring gulls and gannets also occur.

Kentish plover nesting on the beach at Porto Santo

PEACE AND QUIET

An Atlantic sperm whale crests the surface

Porto Santo

The only other inhabited island in the archipelago.
Porto Santo can be visited either on a day trip or for a longer stay. If crossing from Madeira by boat, be sure to watch for seabirds, dolphins and even whales. Arguably the most attractive feature of the island is the sandy beach which runs along the entire length of the southern shore. Kentish plovers are sometimes seen on the beach and a good range of sand dune plants can be found. Look for snails among the dunes – during the summer months they sometimes collect in large, dormant groups on the vegetation, a process known as aestivation.

Prainha

Near Caniçal in the east of the island.
Prainha is the site of the only natural sandy beach on Madeira. Search the strandline for shells and tideline debris. Sand dune plants colonise the shifting terrain as you move away from the sea.

Santa Cruz

Town on the southeast coast.
The coastal cliffs between Santa Cruz and Machico are spectacular and are home to interesting birds such as rock pigeons, plain swifts and pallid swifts. Both species of swift are aerobatic insect feeders and Madeira is one of the few places in the world where birdwatchers can see plain swifts easily.

Sea Life

The seas surrounding Madeira are extremely productive and full of marine life. They provide rich fishing grounds not only for man but also for a wealth of seabirds as well as marine mammals. Although some of these can be seen from the shore, a boat trip will provide the best opportunities for observation. Several species of petrels and shearwaters live and breed around Madeira. Look for tiny Madeiran petrels pattering over the surface of the water while soft-plumaged and Bulwer's petrels and Cory's, Manx and little shearwaters are more powerful fliers. In the winter months they may be joined by gannets – large, white seabirds that feed by plunging into the water.
Several species of whale and dolphin occur in the waters off Madeira although a good deal of luck, as well as calm seas, is needed to see them. Common dolphins and pilot whales are regularly seen and there is even a chance of encountering a sperm whale in deeper water.

Practical

This section (with the yellow band) includes food, drink, shopping, accommodation, nightlife, tight budget, special events etc.

FOOD AND DRINK

The two most common words on Madeiran menus – both easily confused by first-time visitors to the islands – are *espada* and *espetada*. Learn these, and you will know the two ingredients at the heart of Madeiran cuisine.

Espada and Fish Dishes
Espada, or scabbard fish, is a long, black eel-like fish, around 3ft (1m) long with a white, flaky flesh. They live at great depths and are caught only off Madeira and Japan. With their large eyes and sharp teeth, *espada* look extraordinarily ugly and unappetising, but in fact they taste delicious. The fish is cooked in numerous ways – perhaps most successfully when poached in white wine or fried with bananas.

For fish generally, Funchal and Câmara de Lobos offer the widest choice of menus – besides *espada*, the other principal locally caught fish is tuna (*atum*), served as meaty steaks either grilled (*grelhado*) or fried (*frito*) and served with slices of lemon. You may also encounter *bodião* (parrot fish),

garoupa (grouper), *salmonete* (red mullet) and *espadarte* (swordfish, sometimes smoked and served as a starter). Rather than let you worry about names, the best fish restaurants will have their catch out on display – you simply point to your choice, which is sold by weight. Don't be afraid to ask for a large fish to be divided between two.

Many traditional Portuguese specialities can be enjoyed on Madeira too, such as the rich fish soup called *caldeirada*, dishes made with *bacalhau*, dried cod, and *caldo verde*, a soup made with cabbage, potatoes and onions. As on the

Espada, or scabbard fish

FOOD AND DRINK

mainland, servings are often large and accompanied, almost without fail, by boiled potatoes, tinned vegetables and rice.

Espetada and Meat Dishes

A common sight at picnics and festivals, *espetada* is a simple country dish that the Madeirans have elevated into something of an art form. It consists of a skewer, traditionally made of laurel wood but now more usually of metal, holding cubes of meat, normally beef, that is cooked over an open wood fire scented with laurel twigs. Garlic, onions, tomatoes and peppers are sometimes added to the skewer. In restaurants *espetada* is often served hung before your eyes on metal hooks.

In general, the most enjoyable *espetada* meals are to be found inland, in the mountain villages and in the purpose-built restaurants catering to day trippers from Funchal.

Beef (*bife*), pork (*porco*) and chicken (*frango*) frequently feature on menus – the tastiest dishes are often those where the meat is cooked on a wood fire or has been marinated. Some bars and restaurants on Porto Santo occasionally serve local *cabrito assado* (roast kid). Posh Madeiran restaurants are also fond of serving meat *flambé*.

For snacks, many bars can knock up a *prego no prato* (a small steak) in a few minutes. In the country these are often served in rolls made from *bolo de caco*, a delicious local bread cooked on top of a hot stone oven which is sometimes served warm with butter, herbs and garlic. Another legacy from the past is *milho frito*, fried cornmeal – once a staple of the Madeiran diet but now served, often in small cubes, as a somewhat bland accompaniment to main dishes.

Puddings and Cakes

The choice of desserts on Madeira invariably swings between *pudim* – varying types of caramel pudding – and ice cream, including delicious filled-fruit varieties in which halved oranges or other fruit are stuffed with ice cream of the same flavour. The island's forte, though, is cakes – it is wisest to adjourn to a *pastelaria* (pastry shop) or bar for this course. The most common is *bolo do mel*, a dark, rich fruit cake made with molasses and spices. It can be bought in supermarkets, but is also made at home – particularly at Christmas when age-old recipes are used in which the richer versions can have over twenty ingredients. Madeira cake – the light, sandy coloured sponge so popular with the English middle classes – is a 19th-century British creation. It is still served by some hotels, principally to guests whose idea of complete happiness is to sit on a verandah in Madeira with a glass of Madeira in one hand and piece of Madeira cake in the other.

The Madeirans grow a wonderful range of tropical fruits, some now exported by air to Europe. These are displayed daily in Funchal's main market, the Mercado dos

Island produce in the market

Lavradores. You may already be familiar with avocados, kiwi fruits, mangoes, papayas and figs – even custard apples and guavas – but when was the last time you feasted on such exotic curiosities as passion fruit, pittanga, loquat or tomarillo?

Madeira Wine

The islands' most famous product, Madeira wine, has been an integral part of the Madeiran economy since the early days of colonisation. At the instigation of Prince Henry the Navigator, vines were shipped over from Crete and soon thrived in the island's mild climate and rich soils. Originally intended for the settlers' own consumption, demand for the wine grew as a result of Madeira's strategic position on the world's shipping routes. Then known as malvasia or malmsey, the wine was dark, sweet and strong – the ancestor of today's Malmsey, one of four types of madeira wine now produced.

In the 18th century, as more Madeira was being exported, the wine was fortified with grape brandy to help it travel. The shippers were surprised to discover that, unlike other wines, the quality of Madeira was improved by long sea voyages through the intense heat of the Tropics. At first merchants simply sent their wine on long roundabout voyages to mature, but in time methods were found to reproduce the same effect artificially. These have evolved into the *estufagem* system, still in use today. After harvesting and fermentation, the wine is stored in vats and casks and kept in hothouses (*estufas*) at a temperature of at least 45°C (113°F) for at least three months. Once it has cooled, the wine is then matured conventionally in oak casks. Madeira travels well and keeps well – good reasons, as if you

FOOD AND DRINK

needed further convincing, for taking some of these fine wines home with you. Use your time on Madeira to sample the four varieties available – not only in a tasting bar, but with the appropriate course of a meal. As each wine lodge produces its own subtle blends, there is a lot of research to be done. If you need a starting point, try a bottle of Blandy's Rainwater. These are the four main types of Madeira that you will encounter:

● Sercial is the driest, palest madeira, light-bodied and ideal as an aperitif. It is often served chilled.

● Verdelho is medium-dry, with more body than a Sercial and a distinct tang. It is a versatile wine, good as an apéritif or for general drinking.

● Bual is considered a medium-rich madeira, full-bodied and slightly fruity. It is normally served with cheeses and desserts.

● Malmsey is dark, rich and sweet, a natural dessert wine that can also be served as a liqueur to round off a good meal.

Other Drinks

Aside from Madeira wine, the only other wine made here on a commercial basis is Altarlic Rosé, made by the Madeira Wine Company. Many red and white table wines are also produced for purely local consumption. These range from the rough and strong to the quite palatable – try an experimental glass (copo) of vinho da casa (house wine) first, before ordering a whole carafe. Wines imported from mainland Portugal are a reliable

The dust of age on distinguished Madeira wines

alternative – robust oakwood and vanilla flavoured reds from the Dão region, or the fruitier Bairrada, all go well with *espeteda* and other meat dishes. White wines, such as the light, dry Bucelas or the ever popular Vinho Verde, a young, slightly sparkling wine from the northernmost part of Portugal, are ideal companions to Madeiran fish or seafood.

The local beer (*cerveja*) brewed on Madeira is the 'Coral' brand and quite acceptable. Imported beers tend to be expensive. For something stronger, the Madeirans have been distilling spirits from their sugar cane for centuries. Today these are made into various *aguardentes* – notably *branquinha* with a stick of sugar cane inside the bottle, and *poncha*, a concoction of sugar-cane rum plus brandy, lemon and honey. The islands' exotic fruits are also used to flavour an extraordinary range of sweet liqueurs – *maracujá* (passion fruit) is one of the most popular, with others made from custard apples, bananas, aniseed, cherries, almonds and tangerines.

For non-alcoholic drinks, freshly squeezed orange juice (*sumo de laranja*) is available in many bars, with a variety of other exotic fruit juices sold in tins or cartons. Tea is *chá* and coffee *café* – with milk, *com leite*. While the water on Madeira is safe to drink, most visitors stick to bottled mineral water – some of this comes from a natural spring on Porto Santo. Water (*água*) is available either with bubbles, *com gáz*, or without, *sem gáz*.

SHOPPING

Prices and Tax

As many goods have to be imported to Madeira, the cost of day-to-day items, including brand-named food and drink, toiletries and petrol, will be slightly higher than in mainland Europe. In shops and supermarkets there are fixed prices, but in markets and roadside stalls you may be able to strike a bargain.

Visitors from countries outside the European Community can take advantage of shops displaying a 'Tax-Free Shopping' sticker. So long as the item you purchase costs 11,200 escudos or more, you can request a tax-free cheque from the retailer which will give you a refund of between 10 and 20 per cent of the price. This cheque can be exchanged for cash (in Portuguese escudos) at Santa Catarina airport, or you can apply to have the money refunded by credit card or international cheque.

Souvenirs

Madeiran souvenir shops take their inspiration from the island's folklore and do their utmost to ensure that every visitor flies home dressed from head to toe in local costume. If you are not up to an embroidered waistcoat or a pair of *botas* (leather boots with a red stripe), you might succumb to a straw hat as worn by Monte's toboggan drivers or the cosily ear-flapped bobble hats still worn by many workers.

Knitted garments, whether

made by hand or in a factory, are good value. Thick woollen jumpers, gloves and long socks – suitable for both walkers and Father Christmas – are all worth a browse.

Dolls in Madeiran costume, musical instruments such as the castanet-crowded *brinquinho*, old Madeira wine labels or miniatures of Madeira wines and the island's various *aguardentes* and exotic liqueurs all make interesting presents. *Bolo de mel* fruit cake is sold in supermarkets and *pastelarias*, and some shops sell homemade sweets made from eucalyptus and fennel.

Flowers are such a popular gift to bring back from Madeira that airline staff seem to have had special training in accommodating bouquet-laden passengers. The most enjoyable place to buy them is in Funchal's main market, the Mercado dos Lavradores, but it is better to pay more at a florists if you want them wrapped and boxed for safe transportation. Many of the top hotels have a flower shop and there is a small one at Santa Catarina airport. They are not cheap, but flowers are the best way to remember Madeira.

Handicrafts

The worldwide reputation of Madeiran embroidery (*bordados*) is the fruit of a philanthropic enterprise set up on the island in the 1850s. At a time when the island's vines were struck by disease, an English resident, Elizabeth Phelps, encouraged Madeiran women to take up embroidery.

A ready market for their work was found on the tea-tables of Victorian England, and a cottage industry developed that has since given employment to thousands of islanders.

Today the best place to see and buy this exquisite handiwork is in the large factory showrooms in Funchal where the articles are checked, washed, ironed and packaged. If you are after a new cloth for your dining table be prepared for a price shock; there are, however, plenty of smaller items for sale, such as

blouses, children's clothing and handkerchiefs. Genuine garments will always have a little tag fixed to them – a seal of approval from IBTAM, the authority that regulates the islands' handicraft industries. A similar commercial expansion of traditional crafts took place in the 1930s when a German family, the Kiekebens, organised the production of tapestries and other needlework articles on Madeira. These can be very expensive, but cheaper do-it-yourself kits are

The most enjoyable place to buy flowers is in Funchal's market

sold too.

The most widely available Madeiran handicraft is wickerwork, mainly made around Camacha. Shopping baskets, plant-holders and sets of trays are popular buys. Look out, too, for thick dark leatherwork, such as the stationery wallets, bottle holders, footwear and bags made by Artecouro. For something rare but affordable, you can buy paper-knives, model boats and scrimshaws carved from old supplies of whalebone by the redundant whalers in the port of Caniçal.

Wine

Funchal's wine lodges work hard to suit their customers' tastes, and there can be few visitors who leave Madeira without taking home at least a bottle or two of its renowned wine. Normally your first few samples will be free or included in the price of a tour; after that, or for vintage Madeiras, you will be expected to pay.

If you want to ship back several cases you can do so with ease: the Madeirans have been doing this for centuries. One of the joys of their wine is that it travels and keeps so well.

Many visitors buy vintage Madeiras for a special occasion, or as a bequest to the grandchildren – consider the pleasure of opening a wine bottled the year you were born. Some purchases are made with half an eye on investment – an 1822 bottle of Blandys Verdelho can fetch almost £2,000 (US$ 3,000) at auction, so who knows what a 1990s Boal could be worth a century on?

With such possibilities in mind, you should conduct your research at leisure. Only limited quantities of Madeira can be produced, the demand is high and constant, so prices are high. The wines are sold once they are three years old, though a quality Madeira will generally be at least ten. Those over 20 years old can be considered vintage.

ACCOMMODATION

Madeira has always had top quality accommodation. The first tourists to visit the islands in the mid-19th century were sophisticated travellers who arrived by sea with an entourage of companions and servants and barrow-loads of luggage and furniture. Although Funchal had a few hotels by then, most visitors stayed in the hills above the town where luxurious *quintas* with their own walled grounds and

housekeepers could be rented. One leading *quinta*-manager was William Reid, who made a Monopoly-like progress around Funchal creating new hotels, including the distinguished Reid's Hotel, opened in 1891. A century on, Reid's (see page 34) is still the most refined place to stay on the island, while modern 5-star hotels, such as the Savoy, the Carlton (see page 34) and the Madeira Palácio, are evidence that the Madeirans intend to keep things top class. Hotels like

these employ huge numbers of staff and take pride in the personal service they offer their guests. If you can afford to stay at this level, you should have few complaints.

After these, and sometimes equally well-appointed, comes a galaxy of 3 and 4-star hotels in which the majority of visitors stay (for details of specific hotels, see pages 34–5 and other entries in the **What to See** section). These

The modern and luxurious 5-star Madeira Palácio hotel

ACCOMMODATION

range from predictable multistorey tower blocks grouped round a pool, to new, people-friendly low-rise apartment complexes with their own integrated shopping, dining and entertainment centres. While some of the older hotels in Funchal and Machico can seem the worse for wear, those currently being built around Madeira and on Porto Santo are of an excellent standard. Virtually all the hotels in Funchal have a swimming pool (sometimes on the roof) and many rooms have a balcony. If you are not happy with the room you are given, ask to see another – most of the hotels in Madeira are large and only completely full in high season, so a choice should be possible. Smaller hotels are variously described as *pensãos*, *estalagems*, *albergarias* and *residências*. These have fewer facilities but are still well furnished. They may be located above a shop or restaurant, and often they are the only type of accommodation available in the villages outside of Funchal. For something different, *quinta*-style accommodation has been making something of a comeback in recent years. Several manor houses in and around Funchal have been converted into hotels, such as the 28-bedroom Quinta Perestrello, Rua Dr Pita 3, Funchal (tel: 763720) and the 68-bedroom Quinta da Bela Vista, Caminho Avista Navios 4, Funchal (tel: 764144). Equipped with antiques, mature gardens and satellite TV, they offer an appealing blend of modern comforts and period character. Even more distinctive are Madeira's two *pousadas*, government-owned inns that are part of a chain dotted throughout Portugal and intended to attract tourists to scenic parts of the country they might not normally visit. The Pousada dos Vinháticos (page 59) and the Pousada do Pico do Arieiro (page 61) have both been built in Madeira's mountainous centre and are ideal for a night or two of isolated luxury.

Self-catering
There are apartment hotels in Funchal and on Porto Santo where the rooms have kitchen facilities. Villas and private houses can also be rented.

All Portuguese hotels are star-rated from one to five, although in Madeira, as elsewhere, the system can be misleading. A 3-star hotel may well turn out to be preferable to the 4-star next door – it is just that the latter has installed a mini-bar or some other facility to qualify for the higher rating. If, dying of thirst, you open your mini-bar and find it has not been switched on, you will understand this point a little further. Hotels are supposed to display the prices of their rooms, but not all do and you should check the rate charged on arrival. Prices are charged per double room, and usually include a continental breakfast.

For ideas on cheaper accommodation see **Tight Budget**, page 106.

CULTURE, ENTERTAINMENT AND NIGHTLIFE

The top hotels in Funchal, such as the Savoy, the Madeira Carlton and the Casino Park, all have nightclubs or discos and a busy entertainments programme – you do not have to be a guest to gain admission (see page 34 for addresses). Other hotels organise excursions to their regular theme nights, which usually include dinner and a floorshow or folk dancing. Details are advertised in the free English newspaper *Madeira Island*

Showtime at the Casino Park Hotel – a popular nightspot

WEATHER AND WHEN TO GO

Bulletin. The larger hotels put on their own entertainment too, which can range from karaoke and guitar music to magic shows and quiz nights. Folklore evenings, with Madeiran dancers and musicians, are a frequent attraction, along with the fatalistic songs of *fado*, a plaintive music that originated in Lisbon but which is now found throughout Portugal.

For something less engineered head for the Old Town. Here the bars and restaurants offer various combinations of fish, folklore and *fado*, or, if you prefer, cheap drinks and loud music. Other nocturnal nuclei are the sophisticated piano and cocktail bars around Rua da Imperiatriz D Amélia, and the bars and floating restaurants of the marina. Madeira has one casino, at the Casino Park Hotel (see page 34).

Outside Funchal the action is limited to the main hotels in Machico, Caniço de Baixa and, on Porto Santo, the discos of Vila Baleira (see page 84). Go anywhere else and you will find what you may consider to be preferable – just the sound of the waves and the light of the stars.

WEATHER AND WHEN TO GO

Be under no illusions: rain is always a possibility on Madeira. Sometimes it takes the form of a gentle anointing dew that you hardly notice, at other times a majestic downpour that makes the countryside memorably fragrant. One day you will be convinced by the thunderous skies above that Armageddon is imminent, but all that comes is a humid warmth and a soft breeze through the flowers. On another occasion a sudden squall will rush in from the sea, soaking everything in minutes, then vanish leaving a consolatory rainbow arching over wave-pounded rocks. Having said this, the Madeiran climate is remarkable for its consistency throughout the year. The weather is invariably warm, wet and sunny, with average annual temperatures an amicable 16–22°C (61–72°F). Sea temperatures,

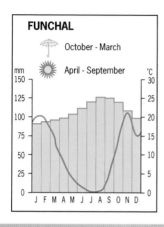

FUNCHAL

October - March

April - September

warmed by the Gulf Stream, range from 21°C (71°F) in summer to 17°C (63°F) in winter. March is a particularly wet month, but in the summer months there is little rain. The southern coast of Madeira gets the most sun, though Porto Santo, being low and exposed, gets even more. Between December and April the temperature steadily increases, and the summer months can get very humid – fortunately Monte,

After the storm – rainbow over Madeira's central mountains

WEATHER AND WHEN TO GO

Santo António da Serra and the hills encircling Funchal offer cool forests and refreshing mountain air. Bear in mind that on Madeira an exhilarating variety of weather can occur simultaneously in different parts of the island. It may be snowing on Pico do Arieiro but blazing hot in Machico, or drizzling in Funchal but gloriously sunny above the clouds on Paúl da Serra.

Between June and September the islands are popular with visitors from mainland Portugal, while in August the beach on Porto Santo is a favourite destination for families from Madeira. Most foreign visitors to the islands come in winter, with hotels virtually full for Christmas and New Year.

What to Take and Wear

After much contemplation, Reid's Hotel recently bowed to modern times and lifted its requirement that men should wear dinner jackets while dining in its *à la carte* restaurant (jacket and tie are still compulsory). Nevertheless, many guests staying in Madeira's top hotels still like to dress for dinner, and there is always a good show of tuxedos and ballgowns for gala nights and Christmas parties. In Funchal's smarter hotel restaurants men are expected to wear a jacket and tie.

For sightseeing and general day-to-day wear, comfortable casual clothes are best. Although Madeira rarely seems cold to visitors from northern Europe, if the sun is lost in cloud, or skulking behind the mountains, you will want a jumper or jacket to hand. Stout, flat shoes should be worn in Funchal, where the streets and squares are frequently paved with decorative black and white pebbles – lovely to look at but adding further pressure to feet already made weary by steep hills, cobblestones and tiny streets clogged with traffic. When travelling inland, which inevitably means climbing to considerable altitudes, take a warm sweater and windproof coat. It is not for the sake of fashion that the local farmers choose to wear knitted bobble hats with long earflaps. Even though the sun is out, there can be cold winds on Paúl da Serra and at Pico do Arieiro and Achada do Teixeira. In winter these peaks are sometimes capped with snow or surrounded by chilling mists, so gloves, scarf and a hat are advisable.

● If you are walking, whether along the *levadas* or elsewhere, try to take clothes you can adjust to suit the varying temperatures you will undoubtedly meet. Always take an anorak or waterproof coat and strong shoes or walking boots that have a good grip. You should also carry a torch (vital if you are going through tunnels), compass, sun hat, sunglasses, maps, guide book and something to eat and drink.

● There are no dangerous animals or reptiles on Madeira and insect bites are rarely a problem. However a good suntan cream is essential.

● If you plan to take a lot of photographs it is best to bring your film with you. Most types of film can be bought in Funchal, but elsewhere the choice is limited. Try to avoid buying film from stalls and souvenir kiosks where it may be out of date or have spent a long time exposed to strong sunlight.

HOW TO BE A LOCAL

The *Madeira Island Bulletin* occasionally publishes tongue-in-cheek advice to its readers on the hazardous world of Madeiran body language. Scratch your throat and you have signalled for a glass of wine, yawn and you will be deemed to be not sleepy but hungry. If another car tries to take your parking space, just waggle your finger like a metronome to say 'No'! Try to remember that palms down means 'stop', but palms down with fingertips pointing up means 'I don't know'.

There is no need to practice these gesticulations in your hotel bathroom before venturing onto the streets. They were born on a sleepy island where people once signalled by hand across hill and valley, boat and shore. Gone are the days when, if a man was talking to a woman in a headscarf, he had to take care. If the scarf was tied one way she would be married, if not it could be his lucky day. Despite the intrusions of the modern world, life here remains civilized and unhurried, and the Madeirans maintain an old-fashioned respect for common courtesies. So don't worry if every time you pass someone they start pulling on an ear. It only means 'very good'.

Typical hat worn by local farmers

CHILDREN

The Madeirans love children. Turn up at a restaurant with a baby or toddler and in a matter of minutes the staff will have whisked Junior off to the kitchen for some serious adulation. Visit the market or a park and your offspring will be heralded with smiles – not just from aspirant and nostalgic mothers, but from men too. Waiters, taxi drivers, young lads on motorbikes, old boys on benches – they will all stop to admire and enjoy your little angel.

Despite this touching welcome, Madeira is unlikely to be your child's favourite holiday destination. While most hotels have swimming pools, or access to artificial seawater pools nearby, the islands have only one good sandy beach, on Porto Santo. This is safe and spacious, but there is no other amusement for youngsters on the island – and if your child gets travel sick (or you, for that matter) it is best to fly to the island as the sea crossing can be rough and nauseous. Furthermore, most visitors to Madeira are middle-aged or older, and the entertainments available reflect the tastes of this mature audience. Having said that, if your child can stay awake, he or she may enjoy the floorshows, cabarets and magic shows put on regularly by the hotels, which will also have table tennis, videos, indoor games and other sports facilities. There are also a good number of parks, gardens and picnic sites around the island. In Funchal, sights of particular appeal to young children are the small aquarium in the Museu Municipal and the Jardim dos Loiros (Parrot Park) next to the Jardim Botânico. The Quinta Magnólia park and the Jardim de Santa Catarina have children's play facilities. As Madeira has few child visitors, the provisions made for them are limited so bear in mind the following points:

● Car rental companies have only a few child seats and you should double-check when booking or take your own.

● Not all hotels and restaurants have high chairs, so if you have your own screw-on type you should take it.

● Large hotels can provide cots, but check their safety before using them.

● In older hotels, some lifts do not have internal doors, so extra vigilance is required when using them.

● Dried milk formula, nappies and baby food can be bought on the islands but since these are very expensive (or a different brand to those you are used to) it is better to bring your own supplies.

TIGHT BUDGET

Madeira is not an ideal destination for budget travellers. The islands have a long tradition of playing host to the well-heeled holidaymaker, and have never embraced the cheap and cheerful style of tourism found in the Canary Islands and various Mediterranean resorts. The majority of hotels are in the 4 and 5-star class, car hire is expensive, and the cost of living is at least as high as that in the rest of Europe.

Here are a few tips on how to enjoy Madeira on a limited budget:

● Book a package holiday out of season, for example in early January. Further savings can often be made if you are prepared to travel at the last minute.

● Stay in a 3-star hotel with half-board, and take coach excursions rather than hire a car.

● Many parts of the islands can also be reached by bus – fares are cheap but it can be difficult to secure a trustworthy timetable.

● Generally, the further you get from Funchal the cheaper things will be. Nearly all the main villages now have pensions (pensãos), many newly built and offering modest, clean accommodation at moderate prices. If you

All dressed up for the Carnival parade on Shrove Tuesday

speak Portuguese you may be able to rent a room in a family house. Unfortunately it is now no longer possible for visitors to use the government rest houses built in the interior of the island. There are only two official campsites on Madeira, in Porto Moniz (see page 54) and on Porto Santo (see page 82).

• In Funchal the Old Town offers the best prospects for a cheap meal – try the *prato do dia* (dish of the day) in the bars and restaurants along Rua de Santa Maria.

• If you need to buy fresh food, visit the Mercado dos Lavradores late in the afternoon when the price of unsold produce begins to fall.

SPECIAL EVENTS

Madeira maintains a busy festive calendar. Hardly a week goes by without something happening somewhere on the islands. If it is not a local *festa* in honour of the village's patron saint, it is a public holiday, or an agricultural fair, or an international flower festival. On a small island such celebrations are all-consuming family affairs that are the result of weeks of planning and preparation. Some are rooted in the islanders' strong religious traditions, while others are folkloric events designed to encourage tourism.

The best *festas* are inevitably those you just come across – you will know when one is on because the roads are full of pick-up trucks loaded with men in suits and hats. Suddenly women are marching down the road bearing specially made

SPECIAL EVENTS

cakes, and teams of workers erecting *espetada* (kebab) stalls in the village square. In the churches, decorated with stunning displays of local flowers, families with immaculately dressed children arrive to attend religious services, while devout processions weave through streets draped with flags and banners. At night the entire village is wrapped in coloured lights, strung from bandstand to bar to palm tree and post office, as chattering Madeirans wait for the sky to fill with fireworks.

Carnival In February or early March, Madeira's carnival takes place in Funchal and in towns and villages all around the islands. As with pre-Lenten celebrations held throughout the world, the carnival is a chance to dress up and let go, with costumed parades, bands, floats and fireworks. The main events take place over a long weekend, with an allegorical parade on the Saturday and a fun parade on Shrove Tuesday.

Flower Festival Over a weekend in April or May, Madeira celebrates its spectacular flora with displays, exhibitions and parades.

Music Festival At the end of May and during June a season of classical musical concerts is staged by local and guest orchestras, with Funchal's cathedral and theatre as the principal venues.

Madeira Wine Rally In early August an international car rally is held. This always attracts many visitors who come to watch drivers tackle Madeira's challenging roads.

Nossa Senhora do Monte On the Feast of Assumption (15 August), the most important religious celebration on Madeira takes place in Monte. Pilgrims come from all over the island to honour the islands' patron saint, praying and singing as they climb the steps to the church.

Grape Harvest Festival In September, another year in the long history of Madeiran wine making is honoured with a week of viticultural events, including grape-treading, tasting sessions and exhibitions.

Christmas Celebrations begin on 8 December with the planting of lentils, chickpeas and corn in small pots. Their green shoots are an essential feature of the elaborate Nativity scenes the Madeirans construct in churches, shops, hotels and village squares throughout the islands. By 16 December these exhibitions are in place and Funchal is a blaze of Christmas lights. On 23 December the Mercado dos Lavradores stays open all night for Christmas shoppers, with Midnight Mass the following evening an important feature of the Christmas programme.

New Year's Eve This is the highpoint of the year's festivities and one of the best firework celebrations in the world. Great journeys are made to be in Funchal on this night – by the cruise liners who schedule their voyages to join the lines of illuminated vessels encircling Funchal Bay, by tourists jetting in from as far away as Scandinavia and Canada, by Madeiran emigrants returning from overseas to visit their relatives, by farmers and their families who drive in trucks across the island to get a mountain-top view.

As the old year fades, every possible light in Funchal is turned on. People gather outside their front doors, on roadsides, terraces and hotel roofs, clutching glasses of champagne and slices of *bolo de mel*. At the stroke of midnight Funchal erupts with the sound of rockets, ships' sirens and cheering revellers as the new year begins.

SPORT

Despite its small size, Madeira has plenty to keep the sports-minded visitor busy. Your first point of inquiry should be your hotel reception, since many of the islands' facilities belong to hotels or are closely associated with them.

Diving In Funchal snorkeling and scuba-diving can be arranged through the Savoy Hotel (tel: 222031). There is a diving centre in Caniço de Baixa (see page 72) – contact the Roca Mar hotel (tel: 933334). On Porto Santo contact Urs Moser Diving Centre, Rua João Gonçalves Zarco 5, Vila Baleira (tel: 982162).

Fishing Big game fishing is well established on Madeira – swordfish, marlin, shark and tuna are some of the prizes to be won from its waters. Charters are normally for four or seven hours with a maximum of four people fishing. Trips can be arranged through Turipesca (tel: 231063) and Costa do Sol (tel: 238538), both located in

Funchal's Marina.

Football Madeira's premier team, C S Marítimo, is currently in the Portuguese First Division. During the season matches take place on alternate Sunday afternoons at the Estádio dos Barreiros in Funchal, not far from the hotel zone. Two other teams also play in the national league: Nacional and União.

Golf Madeira's principal golf course, Campo Golfe de Madeira (tel: 552345), is sited high up on one of the islands' natural plateaux, Santo António da Serra. Recently extended from 18 to 27 holes, this scenic and challenging course has inspirational views back up to the mountains and out over the Atlantic. In January 1993 Santo António da Serra hosted the first Madeira Open, which attracted top competitors from all over the world. The tournament is contracted to run for three years, and seems certain to put Madeira on the international golfing circuit. A new 18-hole course is due to open in late 1993 at Quinta do Palheiro.

Horseriding Contact the Hotel Estrelícia, Camino Velho da Ajuda (tel: 230131), which organises trips to a local riding club (*hipismo*). On Porto Santo there is a *hipismo* at Quinta dos Profetas, Sítio da Ponta (tel: 983165).

Swimming Apart from hotel swimming pools, the Lido complex, on Rua do Gorgulho, has an Olympic-size pool and a children's pool as well as bars and restaurants (*open*: daily 08.30–19.00hrs in summer; 09.00–18.00hrs in winter). Another lido is currently under

construction in the east end of Funchal.

Non-residents can use the pools of Madeira's grander hotels if they pay an admission fee. This is often quite high, but if you take lunch in the hotel restaurant this is normally waived and you are allowed to use the pool for the whole afternoon.

Tennis The Madeirans are keen on tennis and many hotels have their own tennis courts. You can

Big game fishing is a well-established sport

also play in the grounds of Quinta Magnólia, Rua do Dr Pita, where there are squash courts and a swimming pool.

Watersports On Madeira watersports can be arranged through top hotels such as the Savoy and Madeira Carlton (see page 34). In the summer there is a windsurfing school on the beach at Porto Santo.

Directory

This section (with the biscuit-coloured band) contains day-to-day information, including travel, health and documentation

Contents

Arriving

By Air

TAP Air Portugal, the Portuguese national airline, provides the principal link between Madeira and the outside world. Its scheduled services connect many of the world's major cities to Lisbon, from where there are several flights a day to Funchal. In addition TAP operates direct flights to Madeira from London, Paris, Frankfurt, Milan, Rome, Zurich, Madrid, Porto, Faro, Gran Canaria in the Canary Islands and Ponta Delgada in the Azores.

Funchal is 1 hour and 40 minutes from Lisbon, 3 hours and 40 minutes from London.

Charter flights are a popular alternative. These are normally sold by tour operators as part of an all-inclusive package with hotel or self-catering accommodation. Seat-only deals are available through specialist travel operators – look for their adverts in the travel sections of local and national newspapers.

By Sea

There are no passenger ferry services to Madeira, but the islands are a popular port of call for cruise ships throughout the year. Most voyages are combined with a visit to the Canary Islands and sometimes Morocco. Some companies offer sail/fly packages if you only want to do part of the voyage.

Entry Formalities

Visa and health requirements for visitors to Madeira are the same as those for entering the rest of Portugal. For visits of less than 60 days, visas are not required by passport-holding citizens of European Community countries, the USA, Canada, Australia and New Zealand. No vaccinations are required by visitors arriving from non-infected countries.

Airports

Santa Catarina airport is 13½ miles (22km) east of Funchal, linked by a good, fast road. Its runway is to be extended with the aid of European Community grants. The airport terminal is split into two levels: arrivals at ground level and departures on the first floor. There is a tourist information desk in the arrivals lounge with car hire, bus and taxi services just outside. When flying home, it is best to make your purchases before leaving Funchal as the shops and duty-free facilities in the departures hall only have a small range of goods. On Porto Santo a new terminal is currently under construction to replace the present ancient one, which has minimal facilities.

Transport from the Airport

Taxis are the best means to reach your accommodation. A ride from Santa Catarina to the west of Funchal takes 30 to 45 minutes and costs about 3,500 escudos. Prices to various destinations around the island

are displayed on a notice in the arrivals hall, along with a bus timetable. The number 113 bus goes to the centre of Funchal but the service is irregular. The journey takes 45 minutes and costs about 300 escudos. On Porto Santo, a taxi ride from the airport to Vila Baleira takes 10 minutes and costs about 500 escudos.

Information

Santa Catarina Airport tel: 524972 and 524941.
Porto Santo Airport tel: 982414.

TAP Air Portugal, Avenida das Comunidades Madeirenses 10, Funchal (tel: 239200).

Camping

There are only two official sites on the islands – at Porto Moniz (see page 54) and, on Porto Santo, at Vila Baleira (see page 82).

Car Rental

Try to book your car hire before reaching Madeira, particularly if you are visiting at peak holiday times, such as Christmas, Easter and between

Funchal's Lido complex

July and September. Rental costs are high compared to mainland Portugal and other holiday destinations, but if you want to explore and enjoy the island at your own pace you will need a car for at least two or three days. Most companies will only rent to drivers aged 23 or over with at least a year's driving experience. A valid national or international driving licence is necessary, and a cash deposit or credit card payment

DIRECTORY

in advance is usually required. Value added tax (IVA) of 12 per cent will be added to quoted prices.

Atlas, Rua da Alegria (tel: 223100).

Avis, Largo António Nobre 164 (tel: 764546); Santa Catarina airport (tel: 524392).

Hertz, Rua Ivens 12 (tel: 226026); Santa Catarina airport (tel: 524360).

Moinho, Rua Estêvão de Lencastre, Vila Baleira, Porto Santo (tel: 982780).

Consulates

France: Avenida do Infante 58 (tel: 225514).

Germany: Largo do Phelps 6, 1st floor (tel: 220338).

UK: Avenida do Zarco 2 (tel: 221221).

USA: Avenida Luis de Camões, Edifício Infante Bloco B, Apartamento B, 4th floor (tel: 743429).

Crime

The Madeirans are gentle, family-loving people and their island is one of the safest holiday destinations you can visit. So long as you exercise the vigilance and common-sense precautions you would elsewhere in the world, your time here should be free of trouble. Avoid carrying large sums of money or valuable documents in pockets or handbags, and do not leave important items in unattended cars. Most hotels have safes or deposit boxes.

Begging children can be a nuisance, particularly in Câmara de Lobos, but they soon lose interest if you ignore them.

Customs Regulations

As Madeira is part of the European Community, visitors from its member countries benefit from new regulations introduced on 1st January 1993. The amount of duty-paid goods (those bought in local shops) you can take home from Madeira is only restricted by notional limits, above which you may be asked to prove that your purchases are for personal rather than commercial use. If you are aged 17 or over (and have strong arms) you can bring back 800 cigarettes, 400 cigarillos, 200 cigars, 1 kilo of tobacco, 90 litres of wine, 10 litres of spirits, 20 litres of fortified wines (or 26 bottles of Madeira) and 100 litres of beer. The allowances for goods bought in duty-free shops (in airports and on board ships and planes) are unchanged; they also apply to anyone visiting Madeira from a country outside the European Community. These are 200 cigarettes or 100 cigarillos or 50 cigars or 250gms tobacco, 1 litre of spirits (2 litres if under 38.8° proof) or 2 litres of fortified/sparkling wine plus 2 litres of table wine. Visitors from outside the European Community may also benefit from tax-free shopping allowances (see **Shopping**, page 95).

Disabled Visitors

Facilities for disabled visitors to Madeira are limited. TAP Air Portugal has provisions for

The bustle and colour of Funchal's central market

DIRECTORY

passengers with wheelchairs, and luxury hotels, such as the Savoy (see page 34) and Madeira Palácio, are able to offer accommodation of an acceptable standard, as can the Luamar Hotel on Porto Santo (page 82).

Driving

Driving in Madeira is exhilarating but requires close attention to the road. Steep hills, hairpin bends, mist, tunnels, waterfalls, fallen rocks,

potholes, stray sheep and goats, brakeless lorries and dormant labourers are some of the hazards that await. Some drivers and passengers may find the endless curves of the island's roads make them feel travel sick. Let none of this put you off – if you can tour the island at weekends or holidays the roads will be less busy.

Regulations

Drive on the right-hand side of the road. The speed limit in

One of the world's great hotels, Reid's exudes grandeur

Electricity

220 volts. Sockets take round two-point plugs (Continental European size) so most UK appliances will need an adaptor.

Emergency Telephone Numbers

In any emergency dial 115.
Police: 222022
Fire: 222122
Ambulance: 229115
Red Cross: 741115

Health

Adequate medical insurance is recommended. European Community citizens are entitled to reciprocal medical benefits and should obtain the relevant document before leaving home (in the UK Form E111 is available from main post offices). If you need treatment, this, and your passport, should be presented at the Serviço de Migrantes, Centro do Saúde do Bom Jesus, Rua das Hortas 67, Funchal (tel: 229161). *Open*: Monday–Friday 09.30–12.00 and 14.00–16.00hrs.

Your hotel will be able to supply the name of a local doctor or dentist. Many of the practitioners in Madeira speak English – remember to get a receipt if you intend to make an insurance claim. Outside Funchal, most villages have a Centro de Saúde (Health Centre) where you can seek help. Those with emergency facilities (*urgência*) are at Ribeira Brava, Calheta, São Vicente, Porto Moniz, Santana, Machico and Vila Baleira.

built-up areas is 37mph (60kph) and 56mph (90kph) on other roads. The wearing of seatbelts is compulsory and children under 12 are not allowed in front seats.

Petrol

If you are driving inland make sure you have a full tank before setting off. Stations always have pump attendants and unleaded petrol is usually available. Not all of them accept credit cards.

DIRECTORY

Holidays – Public and Religious

Shops, banks and offices are normally closed on the following holidays. If a holiday falls near a weekend, they may also be closed for part or all of the intervening day.

1 January New Year's Day
February/March Shrove Tuesday
March/April Good Friday
25 April Day of the Revolution
1 May Labour Day
May/June Corpus Christi
10 June National Day
1 July Madeira Day
15 August Assumption
21 August Funchal Day
5 October Republic Day
1 November All Saints'
1 December Independence Day
8 December Immaculate Conception
25 December Christmas Day
26 December St Stephen

Lost Property

If you lose any valuables and wish to make an insurance claim you should report this loss to the police and obtain a written statement. In Funchal there is a lost property office (Polícia de Perdidas & Achados) at Rua João de Deus 7 (tel: 222022).

Media

The free monthly English-language newspaper *Madeira Island Bulletin* is a useful and mildly eccentric amalgam of events, information, local news and reflections on the Madeiran way of life. It can be found in hotels, restaurants and tourist offices around the islands. Madeira has three local daily newspapers, *Diário de Notícias,* the *Jornal da Madeira*, and *Notícias da Madeira,* which all have up-to-date information on the weather, exchange rates, cinema programmes, flight times and bus connections to the airport. A wide range of foreign papers and magazines are flown in to the island and are usually on sale the day after publication. There is an English bookshop, which also stocks some French and German titles, at the Pátio, Rua da Carreira 43, Funchal. Madeira Tourist Radio broadcasts on the FM waveband (96mHz) in the morning and evening in English, French, German and Swedish.

Money Matters

The Portuguese unit of currency is the escudo, which is divided into 100 centavos. A dollar sign is used to separate escudos from centavos, for example 200$50. Banknotes are issued for 500, 1,000, 2,000, 5,000 and 10,000 escudos; coins for $50, 1, 2$50, 5, 10, 20, 50, 100 and 200 escudos. It is best to take a mixture of cash, Eurocheques or travellers' cheques and credit cards with you. Many shops, hotels and restaurants in Funchal accept major credit cards and some banks have automatic cash dispensing machines. Money can be changed at a hotel, bank or *serviço de câmbio* (bureau de change) – remember to take your passport, even for cash transactions.

Opening Times

Banks *Open*: Monday–Friday 08.30–15.00hrs including over the lunch hour. *Câmbios* are open longer hours and on Saturday morning. Money can also be changed in hotels.

Shops and Businesses *Open*: Monday–Friday 09.00–13.00 and 15.00–19.00hrs. Saturday 09.00–13.00hrs. In the tourist areas of Funchal many shops are open longer hours and at weekends.

Restaurants *Open*: 12.00–15.00 and 19.00–22.00hrs.

Museums and Gardens Most museums are closed on Mondays and for lunch between 12.00 or 12.30 and 14.00 or 14.30hrs. If there are adjoining gardens these may remain open through the lunch period.

Pharmacies

If you have a minor ailment, visit a *farmácia*. These dispense both advice and medicine, and usually one of the staff will speak English. *Open*: Monday–Friday 09.00–13.00 and 15.00–19.00hrs. At other times a notice on the door will give details of weekend opening and rotating emergency and night services.

Places of Worship

The Madeirans are Roman Catholic and mass is held regularly in churches all around the islands. In Funchal a service in English is held on Sunday mornings at the Igreja da Penha, behind the Savoy Hotel. There is an English church at Rua do Quebra Costas 18 with services on Wednesday and Sunday mornings, and a Scottish kirk next to the São Francisco gardens with services on Thursday evenings and Sunday mornings. There is a Baptist church at Rua Cidade de Honolulu 9 with services on Sunday evenings.

Police

The police maintain an unobtrusive presence on the

In the Old Town area of Funchal, the Capela do Corpo Santo

DIRECTORY

*Exquisite Madeiran embroidery, a
traditional island craft*

islands. If you need them in a
hurry dial 115. In Funchal
policemen and women wear
dark blue uniforms – you may
see one with a red armband
which indicates that he or she
speaks a foreign language and
is especially tourist-friendly.

Post Office

The easiest main post office
(CTT) to find in Funchal is in
Avenida do Zarco, a minute's
walk up from the statue of
Zarco. As well as the usual
postal services, you can send a
telex or telegram and make
long distance telephone calls
from booths where you pay
when you have finished. There
is another large post office just
off the Rua da Ribeira de São

João, which leads northwest of
Praça do Infante. *Open*:
Monday–Friday
08.30–20.00hrs, Saturday
08.30–12.30hrs.
If you are staying in the hotel
zone there is a post office in the
Lido Sol complex on the south
side of the Estrada Monumental.
Open: Monday–Friday
09.00–19.00hrs.
Most towns and villages have a
post office, but they will be
open for shorter hours. Besides
stamps (*selos*) they sell the
Credifone cards used in public
telephones. Some hotels sell
stamps with their postcards,
and stamps can also be bought
in shops displaying a *correios*
sign. Post boxes vary from red,
British-style pillar boxes to tin
boxes strapped to poles and
even antique holes in a village
wall. Look for the word *Correio*
if in doubt. Some boxes are
blue and marked *Correio Azul* –
these are for express mail and
require extra postage.

Public Transport

Buses

Most parts of Madeira can be
reached by bus (*autocarro*), but
services are timetabled to suit
the needs of the islanders
rather than visitors. Orange
buses serve Funchal, while
other colour combinations roam
elsewhere. There are no
printed timetables currently
available – the best sources of
information are tourist offices
and bus station kiosks. Some of
the more useful routes are:

4   Funchal–Ribeira
      Brava–Ponta do Sol
6   Funchal–Ribeira
      Brava–Encumeada–São

Vicente–Boaventura
7 Funchal–Ribeira Brava
23 Funchal–SantaCruz–
Machico
29 Funchal–Camacha
77 Funchal–Santo António da
Serra
81 Funchal–Curral das Freiras
103 Funchal–Poiso–Ribeiro
Frio–Santana–Boaventura
107 Funchal–Ribeira
Brava–Ponta do Pargo
113 Funchal–Machico–Caniçal
139 Funchal – Porto Moniz
In Funchal the main bus station is on the seafront at the eastern end of Avenida das Comunidades Madeirenses. If you plan to do a lot of bus travel in the town you can buy a seven-day pass for around 2,000 escudos. In Vila Baleira the bus station is at the southern end of Rua Maximiano de Sousa Max, not far from the GALP petrol station.

Taxis
Taxis are painted yellow with a blue stripe and are a convenient and reasonably priced way to travel in Madeira. They can be hailed in the street (a *livre* sign indicates that they are free) or picked up at various taxi ranks around Funchal, for instance in Praça do Município and Avenida Arriaga. Any hotel and most bars will call a taxi for you. If you need to telephone for one yourself:
in Funchal tel: 220911/222000/222500
in Machico tel: 762480
in Vila Baleira tel: 982334.
Within Funchal all taxi journeys are metered, and there are set rates from Santa Catarina

airport to various destinations around the island. Fares are 20 per cent higher between 10pm and 6am and on Sundays and public holidays. There is also a fixed price list for taxi tours of the island which is available at the tourist office (for tours call Central Taxis tel: 230016). Many drivers speak good English and, if you are travelling with others it can be economical to use a taxi to tour parts of the island. With luck, you will be driven in a lovingly tended Mercedes by a worldy-wise driver who knows Madeira inside out. If you want to depart from the standard tours, be sure to negotiate a price first, pointing out the route on a map and agreeing on the number of hours it will take.
In Funchal's hotel zone you may encounter smooth-talking drivers with smart cars soliciting for such tours – these people will charge very high rates and should be avoided. If for some reason you feel you have been overcharged, or poorly treated, yellow taxis have a number displayed on their doors which should be reported to the police.

Boats to Porto Santo
There is a regular passenger service by catamaran between Funchal harbour and Porto do Abrigo in Porto Santo. The crossing takes from 90 to 110 minutes and can be rough at times. In very bad weather sailings may be cancelled.
In winter there is one crossing a day (except Tuesday) with a more frequent service in summer. Details of sailing times

are available from tourist offices, travel agencies and the ship's agents. In summer the schedules can make a day trip to Porto Santo worthwhile. For information:

in Funchal tel: 227020
in Vila Baleira tel: 983565.

Flights to Porto Santo

There are several flights a day between Santa Catarina airport and Porto Santo airport. The service is operated by LAR using small Dornier 228 aircraft. Bookings should be made through TAP Air Portugal (see page 113 for their address in Funchal) or travel agencies. The flight takes 15 minutes and gives good views of Ponta de São Lourenço and Porto Santo.

Telephones

There are numerous phone boxes on Madeira, and many bars have coin-operated or metered telephones for use by the public. A selection of 10, 20 and 50 escudos coins will be enough for local calls. For international calls it is easier to use a Credifone card in a phone box that accepts these. They can be bought in post offices for 500 escudos upwards. You can also visit a main post office to use a telephone booth where you pay at the end of your call. Calls made from a hotel room in Madeira are painfully expensive.

To call another European country from Madeira dial 00 followed by the country code (44 for the UK, 353 for Ireland) then the area code (omitting any

Hats for sale – the typical woollen hat of the island

initial 0) and the local number. To call the USA or Canada dial 097 1 first. To call Australia dial 097 61 and for New Zealand dial 097 64.

Directory Enquiries: 118 (within Madeira)
Operator: 090
International Operator: 099

Time

Between the last Sunday in September and the last Sunday in March the time on Madeira is Greenwich Mean Time (GMT); for the rest of the year it is GMT plus one hour.

Tipping

Tipping is customary but not obligatory – 10 per cent for taxi-drivers and restaurants, 50 to 100 escudos for waiters, porters and maids. Some hotels and restaurants include a service charge in their bills (*serviço incluído*), but people often leave a tip as well.

Toilets

Public conveniences are marked *Senhoras* (women) and either *Homens* or *Senorhes* (men), are often found near central squares. Some are clean and modern while others leave a lot to be desired. Hotels, bars and restaurants offer better facilities – you do not have to be a customer but it is polite to ask first.

Tourist Offices
Overseas

For information on Madeira before you leave home, there are Portuguese National Tourist Offices in many cities around the world, including:
Canada: 60 Bloor St West, Suite 1005, Toronto, Ontario M4W

DIRECTORY

3B8 (tel: 416–921 7376).
Germany: Kaiserstrasse 66–4°,
6000 Frankfurt/N (tel:
69–234094).
Japan: Regency Shinsaka 101,
8–5–8 Akasaka, Minato–Ku,
Tokyo 107 (tel: 3-547 444000).
Portugal: Palácio Foz, Praça dos
Restauradores, 1200 Lisbon (tel:
01–346 3643).
UK: 22-25A Sackville St, London
W1X 1DE (tel: 071–494 1441).
USA: 590 Fifth Avenue, 4th Floor,
New York, NY 10036–4704 (tel:
212–3544403).

Madeira

The main tourist office (*Turismo*)
is in Funchal at Avenida Arriaga
18 (tel: 225658).
Open: Monday–Friday
09.00–20.00hrs, Saturday
09.00–18.00hrs.
There are smaller offices at:
Santa Catarina Airport, in the
arrivals lounge (tel: 524933);
Machico, Edifício Paz, Rua do
Ribeirinho (tel: 965712);
Porto Santo, Edifício da
Delegação do Governo
Regional, Vila Baleira (tel:
982361).

Travel Agencies

Travel agencies can help
arrange car hire, boat trips,
island tours, flights and ferries.
If you want to take a coach or
minibus excursion do not
assume that what your hotel
offers is all that is available.
While such trips all visit the
same destinations, the timing,
routes and prices do vary.
Travel agencies have the best
choice of leaflets advertising
these tours, so shop around to
find the package that suits you
best. Operators normally pick
up passengers from the larger

A quiet siesta

hotels in Funchal. A deposit of
at least 30 per cent is usually
requested when making a
booking.
Blandys, Avenida das
Comunidades Madeirenses 1
(tel: 220162). Day trips to Porto
Santo, jeep safaris with
espetada (kebab) picnics,
levada walks and folklore
evenings.
Madeira Adventure Tours, c/o
João das Freitas Martins Lda,
Avenida das Comunidades
Madeirenses (tel: 221106).
Guided minibus tours with a
maximum of eight people.
Madeira Express, Avenida
Arriaga 38 (tel: 225250).
Minibus tours with taped
commentary.
Madeira Safari, Rua António
José de Almeida (tel: 228684).
Day and half-day trips by jeep
along forest and mountain
tracks, boat trips to Ribeira
Brava.

LANGUAGE

Everyday Phrases

good morning bom dia
good afternoon boa tarde
good night boa noite
please faz favor
thank you obrigado; or, if you are a woman, obrigada
I'd like queria
yes/no sim/não
how much quanto custa?
I'm sorry desculpe
not at all de nada
goodbye adeus
can you direct me to.. pode indicar-me o caminho para...
to the right à direita
to the left à esquerda
do you speak English? fala inglês?
I don't understand não entendo

While Travelling/Sightseeing

airport aeroporto
bathroom quarto de banho
beach praia
bookshop livraria
bread shop padaria
bridge ponte
bus station estação de autocarros
bus stop paragem
cake shop pastelaria
campsite parque de campismo
cathedral sé
chapel capela
chemist farmácia
church igreja
danger risco/perigo
doctor médico
farm quinta
fish shop peixaria
fountain fonte
garage garagem
garden jardím
greengrocer hortaliceiro
house casa
inn estalagem
library biblioteca
left (direction) esquerdo
market mercado
men homens or senorhes
museum museu
palace palácio or paço
park parque
petrol/gasoline gasolina

petrol station posto de gasolina
police station posto de policia
post office correio
quay cais
right (direction) direito
restaurant restaurante or tasca
river ribiera
shower banho de chuveiro
square praça
supermarket supermercado
swimming pool piscina
telephone telefone
telephone kiosk cabina telefónica
theatre teatro
tobacconist tabacaria
tourist information poste de turismo
town centre centro cidade
town hall câmara municipal
women senhoras

Food and Drink

apple macã
breakfast pequeno almoço
lunch almoço
dinner jantar
tea (meal) lanche
the bill a conta
is the service included? o serviço está incluido?
the wine list a lista dos vinhos
beer cerveja
bread pão
cake bolo
cheese queijo
chicken frango
coffee (small black) bica
coffee (white) café con leite
eggs ovos
fish peixe
fruit fruta
ham fiambre
ice cream gelado
lamb anho
milk leite
orange juice sumo d'aranja
pork porco
rice arroz
shellfish mariscos
soup sopa
steak bife
sugar açúcar
tea chà
tuna atum
veal vitela
water (with gas) água (com gaz)

INDEX

INDEX/ACKNOWLEDGEMENTS

Acknowledgements
The Automobile Association wishes to thank the following photographers,
libraries and organisations for their assistance in the preparation of this
book.

Peter Baker took all photographs in this book (© AA Photo Library) except for:

JON WYAND 6 & 38 Funchal, 11 farming the terraces, 45 Monte, 51 agriculture,
59 Pico do Arieiro, 60 Cabo Girão, 65 Santana, 110 fishing, 116/7 Reid's Hotel,
121 hats

MADEIRA TOURIST BOARD 81 Porto Santo, 83 windmill, Porto Santo,
84 Vila Baleira, 110 big game fishing

NATURE PHOTOGRAPHERS LTD (P R Sterry) 87 Painted Lady,
88 Goldfinch, 89 Kentish Plover, 90 Sperm Whale

WYN VOYSEY 4 Botanic Garden, 27 Botanical Gardens, Funchal

The Automobile Association would also like to thank the **Automóvel Club de
Portugal** for their assistance in checking details in the Directory.
The author would like to thank the following organisations and individuals for
their assistance: Portuguese National Tourist Office, London; Direcção Regional
de Turismo, Madeira; TAP Air Portugal; Avis; Alice Prier; Andrew Jones and
Brigid O'Hara.

Series adviser and Copy editor: Christopher Catling
Indexer: Marie Lorimer